Legal Disclaimer

ISBN 978-0-578-12035-5

Printed in the United States of America
2nd Edition, 2014

Christopher J. Monge

CONCEALED CARRY & SELF-DEFENSE INSURANCE EXPERT

Affordable Insurance Solutions, LLC

www.ConcealedCarryInsurance.com

608-663-9800

Sign up online for our

Newsletter today!

Visit our websites at either:

www.ConcealedCarryInsurance.com

OR

www.Self-DefenseInsurance.com

and enter your information online.

You'll get our monthly E-Newsletters that will update you on Self-Defense Insurance, Gun Laws, real-life Armed Citizen Reports, guns, gear and more!

BE SURE TO TELL YOUR FRIENDS AND FAMILY ABOUT US AND TELL THEM TO SIGN UP TOO!

This book is dedicated

to my beautiful wife Jessica…

the love of my life!

TABLE OF CONTENTS

INTRODUCTION

My name is **Chris Monge** (pronounced "M-on-Jee") and I am a Concealed Carry License holder, gun lover, NRA member and Second Amendment supporter! I'm also the #1 Leading Expert in the Self-Defense Insurance field. I know what is needed for a personal insurance program to cover you against legal fees and civil suits stemming from a Self-Defense incident, and I wrote this book to get you informed about what you need.

IF YOU OR SOMEONE YOU KNOW OWNS A GUN, YOU NEED TO READ THIS BOOK CAREFULLY!

By my guesstimate over 80% of gun owners and concealed carry license holders are not insured properly and they don't even know it! Many have never even thought of asking their insurance agent about this and even if they do, *most agents tell them the wrong information because they simply don't know!*

This has become a "super-hot" topic of late, prompting many people into thinking about applying for their concealed carry licenses. Many more already have a license they weren't using and are now starting to carry a weapon because you just never know what may happen.

Let's back up a bit and I'll explain how I got to be the leading expert on Concealed Carry and Self-Defense Insurance coverage and what prompted me to write this book.

The main reason is most insurance companies EXCLUDE *"intentional injuries and intentional acts"* from their policies and pulling the trigger on purpose even if it is for Self-Defense is still an intentional act...**and it won't be covered!** If you have a homeowner's or personal liability umbrella policy that does not add back the language that allows for Self-Defense you are going to be on your own if you are sued over a Self-Defense shooting! As a gun owner and Concealed Carry license holder this just wasn't acceptable for me so I had to see what was out there...

Back to the beginning of my journey...

Living in Wisconsin we were way behind the times in approving a Concealed Carry Law in our state...we were the forty-ninth state to approve it for crying out loud! To be fair, our state legislators did approve the law several times previously but we had a Governor that vetoed it each time leaving us as one of the last two states who wouldn't allow it (he's gone now thankfully). In July, 2011 we did get it passed and now Illinois has finally become the last state to allow some form of concealed carry license.

So...they passed our Concealed Carry law in July 2011 to be in effect on November 1, 2011 and that caused a mad scramble for people to get certified to carry weapons legally. I took my training for both Utah and Wisconsin at the same time in late July and I now hold both licenses and can legally carry a weapon in over thirty states. One of my best friends has a home in Arizona and lives there from January – June each year. He's had a Utah permit for the past few years and he ran across a Firearms Liability Insurance Policy and called me right after our law was passed asking me to research the policy to see if I could offer it to our clients.

So began my journey of learning about Concealed Carry, Self-Defense and how insurance works (or doesn't work) for us. I quickly figured out **there are two moving parts to the Self-Defense equation:**

PART ONE: You have the legal fees you'll incur if you are involved in a Self-Defense shooting because no matter how justified you are – you still need to retain an attorney to go and talk to the DA and get your name cleared…and in the worst case you will have to be able to pay an attorney to defend you in court if the authorities do decide to charge you with a crime (look at what George Zimmerman had to go through)!

PART TWO: You have the civil liability exposure and many states have laws similar to Wisconsin's Castle Doctrine BUT those usually only allow you immunity from prosecution or civil suits if you are in your home, auto or business you own or occupy…so what happens if you are out at a restaurant with your family? You are not covered by the Castle Doctrine and are open to being charged with a crime or sued by your target, their families or bystanders.

There are several different types of insurance policies that will give you coverage for civil liability in a Self-Defense incident and I will review them for you in the relevant order of best/most protection versus the least protection.

The Firearm Liability policy my friend inquired about was similar to several other policies that are currently available and I'll talk about them later in this book. My initial Firearm Liability policy was offered by Lloyd's of London with a $250,000 limit and it could be used as a reimbursement for legal fees or used for civil suits related to a Self-Defense shooting incident, or both, up to the policy limit.

We started marketing the policy heavily and had quite a bit of interest in it from new CCW license holders in Wisconsin. During this time I continued to do research and found several National Property & Casualty Insurance Carriers (and more since) who have "Self-Defense Friendly" language in either their home or personal liability umbrella policies…which was welcome news because these policies have liability limits ranging from $1,000,000 - $5,000,000 which is much better than the $250,000 coverage offered by the Lloyd's of London Firearm Liability policy!

I quickly started using the umbrella policies for the Civil Liability part of the equation to complete our insurance program and because of our marketing I was interviewed for several newspaper articles and television news stories because it was such a hot topic! You can read the stories or watch the clips on our website at **www.ConcealedCarryInsurance.com** if you'd like to see them.

I was using the Lloyd's of London Firearm Liability Policy for the legal fee side of the equation (since no insurance company will pay for you to talk to an Attorney about criminal charges) and then unexpectedly in April, 2012 Lloyd's decided to pull the policy from circulation and we couldn't offer it anymore...

So there I was scrambling to find an alternative for the legal fee side of the equation and low and behold, like they say "when a door closes a window opens" I found the CHLPP program to cover the legal fees which was even BETTER than what I had before! I'll go into more detail on this later in the book.

So...since April, 2012 we have partnered up with the CHLPP program and offer the most comprehensive coverage for both legal fees and civil liability for Concealed Carry license holders and Self-Defense incidents and as far as I can tell we are the only Insurance Agency in the country that offers such a comprehensive program! (In 2013, the CHLPP program merged with Patriot Legal and they are now one in the same.)

CHAPTER 1

The Legal System Perspective

An interview with Attorney Paul Bucher,
Former DA of Waukesha County, Wisconsin and now Criminal Defense Attorney

When I got the idea to write an informative book on Concealed Carry & Self-Defense Insurance it occurred to me that I needed to have a Defense Attorney's perspective (and also a Prosecutor's perspective) on what happens **AFTER** the shooting occurs and what you should expect even if you were totally in the right in a Self-Defense shooting.

I met Paul Bucher after CBS Channel 58 in Milwaukee, WI aired a story about Wisconsin's Concealed Carry law and how it reacts with your homeowner's insurance policy (you can watch it here: **www.concealedcarryinsurance.com**).

Paul was featured in the story along with me and Mark Hinkston who is another Milwaukee-area attorney you'll meet shortly.

Paul Bucher was the Waukesha County District Attorney for twenty-eight years and has since switched over to become a criminal defense attorney—something he is very good at by the way, because of all his years prosecuting criminal cases. He has definitely become my "go-to" guy for a criminal defense attorney and will be the one I call if I am ever involved in a self-defense incident.

I wanted to interview Paul because he brings us the perspective coming from the legal side—both the prosecution and as a defense attorney. This is invaluable information that all firearm owners need to read. I recorded the call and here is the transcript of our phone conversation below in order to preserve his comments and share them with you so you can see where he's coming from.

BE SURE TO TELL YOUR FRIENDS WHO OWN WEAPONS TO READ THIS FOR THEMSELVES.
ALL GUN OWNERS NEED TO KNOW THIS INFORMATION!

CHAPTER 1

Here is a transcript of a phone interview that I did with Paul on what happens after the shots are fired:

Chris Monge:

Paul, as you know I am writing a book about Concealed Carry and Self-Defense insurance and I contacted you for information from the perspective of a Prosecutor and Criminal Defense Attorney. I'm looking for what happens on the legal system end of the equation when you are involved in a shooting, can you explain from an attorney's standpoint what actually happens if you are involved in a self-defense shooting for us?

I know you would have to go talk to an attorney and have dealings with the District Attorney, but can you lay out what happens? I know some experts tell you the first thing you do is call 911 and say you were in a self-defense shooting and then to shut up and call your attorney, but what really happens and what can we expect?

Paul Bucher:

I'm not sure that's sage advice. You know I personally believe anyone who has a Concealed Carry Permit should do live fire drills and practice with the weapon. Buying a firearm is a big step and owning or carrying it without practice is a not a good idea. You need to go through 50-100 rounds or so and practice holding it and know what it feels like to pull the trigger.

But putting that aside, being involved in a self-defense shooting is a very traumatic, emotional incident and as the former District Attorney of Waukesha County (WI) for 28 years, I've been involved in many of those cases — most being police officers but not all and now being involved on the defense side I have been involved in one self-defense shooting case and it is not anything like you see on TV.

I think a lot of people believe you pull the trigger and the bad guy is hit and down he goes or he's picked up and thrown through the window. Well it doesn't happen like that. It's very gruesome and there are body parts and blood and bones and fragments and it's a very, very serious unbelievable incident and the individuals involved are having such an adrenaline rush that I've had people involved that were at point blank range from each other and six to twelve shots were fired and nobody was hit.

It's just you think you can do it but you don't know until you are in that situation. I have several clients on retainer who haven't done anything, but have a firearm and a Concealed Carry permit, and the first thing I told them is to make sure you do the live fire and understand the gun and keep it in a safe place. Number two, if you do have to use a firearm in self-defense you do so with absolute certainty, as absolutely as you can be, that deadly force is necessary.

And even though you may not have to retreat and Wisconsin has the castle doctrine, nobody wants to kill anybody... I personally have a Concealed Carry Permit but I don't want to kill anybody and I hope I never have to use my weapon...and I know they don't use kill, they use terminate the threat instead for the terminology. You have to be certain in your mind that deadly force is absolutely necessary if you are going to use your weapon.

Use whatever terminology you want but five shots center-mass generally is going to correspond to death or if it is a head shot which is what they teach in many classes, is to take a headshot, so do whatever you can to retreat even though you don't have to legally here in Wisconsin.

I'm not going to stand there on principle saying well you know I didn't have to retreat so I shot him...well no I want to retreat, I don't want to shoot anybody if I can avoid it because of the ramifications brought by my actions.

But if it comes to that and you have no choice, it's either him or you and you have to use deadly force, you pull out that firearm and once you pull that firearm and it's out of your holster or wherever you got it from, you're most likely going to shoot.

Something's going to happen, bad things are going to happen and once that finger comes off that weapon and pulls onto the trigger shots are going to be fired. There's a lot that happens and it's a very gruesome situation to see, the adrenaline is incredible.

Verbalization is very important, be very loud because you want everyone to hear...neighbors, anybody that may be listening, in today's world everybody is videotaping something, it's drop the gun drop the gun, get out I'll shoot you, drop the knife, I'll shoot you, I'm afraid, whatever it is, you have to be very loud and people don't think about that.

Whenever I taught police officers these same things, I taught them that sixteen SWAT members emptying out of a van in ninja costumes to hit a house, I would tell them you think nobody is watching? Everybody is watching so you need to verbalize! Verbalization is VERY important!

Secondly is making sure you have target acquisition. I know it is easy to say because I've never been involved in a shooting; I've reviewed dozens of them, dozens and dozens. Target acquisition is very important and thinking about downrange, making sure that if you miss and you probably will, odds are you will, even if they are close to you.

Downrange, what are you going to hit? If I shoot and I miss, I have a .40 Glock and I miss, the bullet is not going to stop, it's going to keep going and hit my neighbor's house.

So I need to be aware of that and I know this is a lot to think about in a nano-second, but think about downrange because that could result in serious consequences for you, not to mention the bad guy is going to be very pissed, and number two you don't know what you just hit.

So target acquisition is important and downrange you have to make sure you have a clear shot and as the lingo goes you terminate the threat. And obviously try to count your rounds...It's easy if you have a semi auto to fire off ten to fifteen rounds in a matter of seconds. People question why did you shoot him seven times? Well I didn't know I shot him seven times...I shot until he dropped his gun.

So you're not going to think about that, but it's a factor when the bad guy is down on the ground...continuing to shoot is not a good idea. You want to kick the weapon away, dial 911, verbalizing to the 911 dispatcher what happened...tell them I felt threatened, I thought he was going to kill me, I had to shoot, oh my god I can't believe this guy was in my house, I was afraid for my family , I was afraid for my life...

You need to do this because self-defense in most states as it is in Wisconsin has two prongs, reasonableness... one is subjective and one is objective. So make sure you verbalize that as much as possible and if you can render first aid...I know it sounds like an oxymoron because you just shot the guy...but trying to render first aid I think goes a long way.

Make sure the bad guy doesn't have access to the weapon, and your weapon is secured, and verbalize, verbalize, verbalize while you are talking to the 911 dispatcher.

The next thing that happens is you're going to have police officers coming from every jurisdiction you can imagine and they won't know who the bad guy is... they have no idea.

They don't know who you are so clearly you want to make sure you don't have your weapon in your hand, and if you have your weapon in your holster, it remains in the holster. If not, put it in a location where the bad guy can't get it and come out with your hands up and go down on your knees, that's the traditional response to a police officer.

Verbalize to the police...I'm the homeowner, I'm the homeowner and I'm not armed. I had to shoot an intruder and I thought he was gong to kill me and I was afraid for my life.

I am not armed, I am not armed...raise your hands and do not in any circumstance have the gun in your hand, if you have a gun in your hand and you turn toward the police to direct whatever type of verbalization you are trying to do they will shoot you.

Don't have the firearm in your hand and that is very important to remember. And verbalize, verbalize, verbalize as loud as you can so everybody can hear it.

Get down on your knees and if necessary get down on the ground and you'll be handcuffed and they are going to take your gun…and that's just the way it goes and you have to expect that's going to happen and that's a reasonable response from the police.

Then they are going to obviously turn to the bad guy and once they identify who's the bad guy and who's the good guy they are going to render medical assistance to the bad guy you shot.

Author's Note: **THIS IS IMPORTANT**

Then comes the Q&A where they are going to want you to tell them — in this highly charged emotional atmosphere where you have nothing but adrenaline in your bloodstream — what happened.

And that's the most dangerous part because people let their guard down and I'm not saying people should lawyer up but look, this guy came into my house, I had no choice, I tried to retreat, I verbalized, I had to shoot him because I felt I had no choice…he was going to kill me.

It is very important to do that, when you get into the details and they will get into them, they will probably take you into custody, and take you down to the police station. This is the time to say, I want to talk to you, I want to explain to you what happened, I want to be truthful and cooperative with you but I'd like to have my lawyer here.

You need to say this because there are potential civil ramifications coming at you and potential criminal ramifications and that's the time to say, I want Paul Bucher here or I want Jane Smith here or Tom Jones here, whoever the lawyer is, to specifically specify by name that is also important and try to get that lawyer down there to discuss the case.

Then of course there is all the aftermath…cleaning up the mess, getting a cleaning company in, calling your insurance company, if they will cover you and the likelihood is they will not unless you have the specific concealed carry coverage.

Most homeowner policies will have an exclusion for these types of things, so making sure you have that insurance coverage and contacting your insurance agency, they are going to want to know what happened and it's important to know you have to cooperate with them or they will deny coverage.

I want to point out it's important to recognize there are two different systems coming together here…the criminal system and the District Attorney are going to look at this case to determine or not if you had that reasonable belief and that's where the verbalization comes in, and secondly was that belief to use deadly force was reasonable objectively.

Or in other words, would a person in the same circumstances use deadly force?

So that's the goal, to have the charging authority make that call that it was done in self-defense, you don't want to have to argue that in front of a jury. You don't want to have to be charged and go through all that expense and a jury because jury's are unpredictable.

So you want to end this and end it quick and you want to end this with the prosecutor making the call that it was a legitimate shoot and you want to get it done as quickly as you can and you want to make sure you've done everything you can to make that possible.

But don't be surprised if you are sued. I'm not an ambulance chaser I'm not out there chasing people to sue them but there are lawyers that are. Especially if you do have insurance and they'll sue you and your insurance company.

It's important to remember not to talk to anybody other than your attorney, your priest, god and your insurance company because they are going to defend you… anybody that has privilege is okay to talk to.

The other thing that is very important because it is a traumatic incident is to get help. To get a therapist to help you deal with what happened because you may think you are fine but you are not fine. Many police officers involved in shootings are reluctant to seek help but after getting therapy they are much better able to handle the situation.

Then it is a matter of circling the wagons and letting your attorney deal with the legal side and letting your insurance company deal with the civil side…

It is a highly traumatic, highly charged situation that is not at all like you see on TV. It is traumatic not dramatic!

Chris Monge:

OK, so my whole book is based on these issues you just described….can you talk about the fees involved for the legal defense?

What is the cost? How long does it take?

Paul Bucher:

Well it all depends.

In the last case I was involved in it took a long time because my client shot an intruder who he thought had a gun but it turned out to be a cell phone. The District Attorney wanted to see if there were fingerprints of my client on the phone so it took quite a while.

It really varies depending on the circumstances. Cooperate and let your lawyer take the lead. It can take a matter of days to a few weeks depending on how complicated the situation is.

I always say to sit back and let your lawyer handle everything and I suggest you should get out of the area for a little bit, get de-briefed, get some help and have your lawyer try to get it shut down as quickly as possible.

As for costs, they can range from $3,500-$5,000 to get your case reviewed and wrapped up but if unfortunately there are charges that do come out of this that figure can go upwards of $20,000 or more.

Self-defense is what we call an affirmative defense or what I call a "but-for" defense..."well I did it BUT...I would not have done it if"...that is something for the jury. If it goes that far down the road and you are in front of a jury, that's not a good place, it's not a good place.

In my opinion, you are best off investing all your resources up front and retain a good attorney to terminate the process as soon as possible so you don't have to go down that road.

I think $3,500-$5,000 is reasonable for what you would expect to pay to get the process complete without being charged, and if you are charged it will be $20,000 or more and that is not unreasonable, probably more because you'll have costs for experts and other witness testimony to help you win your trial.

So, in summary the costs vary widely for a criminal charge and then on the civil liability side you better have a good insurance company that will cover you in the event of a civil suit pertaining to self-defense.

Chris Monge:

That's the problem and the reason for writing this book! Most insurance companies exclude intentional injuries or intentional acts but I have found seven different insurance carriers I represent that are self-defense friendly, I'm sure there are a few more and I'm continuing my search but I have a great mix of carriers already.

I have made it a policy for my agency to only write coverage for concealed carry licensees and gun owners, even if it is only a deer rifle or shotgun with a carrier that has the self defense friendly language. That way if there is an incident you'll know you have your insurance company's policy on your side as long as you are found not guilty of any criminal wrongdoing.

Paul Bucher:

Really, I did not know there were that many carriers that had self-defense friendly language in their policies and I think that is a good thing and this is great you are bringing this to people's attention.

Chris Monge:

We have a really good program put together and the legal fees are covered as well. Have you heard of the CHLPP program?

Paul Bucher:

No I haven't

Chris Monge:

It stands for Carry Handgun License Protection Program and they are a legal fee membership organization. For $129.00 a year you will have all of your legal fees paid directly for you if you are involved in a self-defense shooting incident.

It is not a reimbursement plan and there is no limit to the amount paid on your behalf for legal defense costs stemming from a self-defense shooting while you are a member.

Paul Bucher:

Really! I didn't know that!

Chris Monge:

I'll send you the information on it and you can take a look at it.

Paul Bucher:

Please do – I'm going to get that for myself and I'll be sure to tell other people about the program.

Chris Monge:

So one last question, if you do in fact have to go to trial, how long can you expect a trial to last? I know the George Zimmerman trial will be a circus and I'm assuming in Wisconsin you would be a little less high profile than that one but what would a trial take to complete?

Paul Bucher:

You can assume several days to a week to get a self-defense trial completed in most cases unless it is really in-depth and messy. Generally it should be less than a week to get your trial completed and again that depends on how many expert witnesses are called and how in-depth you get with testimony.

Chris Monge:

OK, well that about wraps it up for me on my end – I think you've given readers a good insight into what happens after you pull the trigger – any last thoughts from you?

Paul Bucher:

Again… just make sure you comply with the officers and make sure you put your gun in a safe place so you don't go to the door with a gun in your hand when the police show up…you don't want to get shot for being stupid.

Then just do everything they say, know they are going to detain you and tell them you want to answer all of their questions but you'd like to have your attorney present to answer in detail and do everything you can to make sure you get the case shut down as quickly as possible.

As long as you are truly justified in your self-defense and you didn't walk up to the guy and put eight shots into him laying on the ground you shouldn't have any problems.

And one last final thought I always tell people to pull their weapon and pull the trigger as a last resort… you don't want to do it unless you feel there is no other option.

Try to move away from the incident if you can and if you can't, make sure you do everything correctly and make sure you sit down with the detectives and the District Attorney with your attorney present and give them all the information on what happened in as clear a manner as you can.

Chris Monge:

OK — thank you Paul for this great information, I really appreciate it.

If you live in the Madison/Milwaukee, WI area and would like to have Paul be your preferred attorney in the case of a Self-Defense incident here is Paul's contact info and a short BIO on his experience:

PAUL E. BUCHER, Attorney-at-Law
W288 N8061 Park Dr., Hartland, WI 53029
(262)538-0277

PERSONAL INFORMATION:

Date of birth: June 21, 1955
Place of birth: Milwaukee, WI
Children: Breanne, Timothy, Christopher, Matthew and Anne

EDUCATIONAL HISTORY:

High School: Pius XI, Milwaukee, WI

College: University of Wisconsin-Milwaukee
- Bachelors of Science Degree . . . . . December 1977
- Dean's List 1976-1977

POST GRADUATE:

Pepperdine University, School of Law, Malibu, CA 1978-1979
- Deans List 1978-1979

Marquette University School of Law, Milwaukee, WI
- Degree of Juris Doctoris . . . . . May, 1981
- Deans List 1980–1981
- Recipient of AM JUR Award for Excellence
- Graduate Studies-University of Wisconsin-Milwaukee
- Political Science, Masters Program

EMPLOYMENT HISTORY:

Bucher Law Group, LLC – Owner and Attorney at Law . . . . . 9/1/10 to current.
Criminal litigation, state and federal, civil litigation, open records/meetings cases, election law, labor/employment law and victimology matters (represent victims of crime in criminal and civil courts)

Gatzke and Ruppelt, S.C. – Attorney at Law . . . . . January 2007 to 8/31/10
Civil litigation, criminal defense, government relations, open records, open meetings, victimology, labor law

Waukesha County District Attorney: District Attorney for Waukesha County . . March 1988 to January 2007
- Supervise and manage a large public law firm in the County. Legal staff of 19 and support and investigative staff of 35. Annual budget of $2,000,000

Assistant District Attorney: Waukesha County District Attorney's Office . . . . January 1983 to March 1988

Executive Assistant/Legal Counsel: State Senator Susan Engeleiter

TEACHING EXPERIENCE:

Certified Instructor, Wisconsin Department of Justice
- Search and Seizure
- Arrest
- Constitutional law

Certified Instructor, Milwaukee Area Technical College
- Business Law . . . . . (Outreach Instructor 2002)
- Business Law 102 . . . . . (Fall Semester 2003)

Law Enforcement Instructor
- Waukesha County Technical College

Carroll College
- Political Science
- Public Administration
- Criminal Law/Procedure

ITT Institute
- Political Science
- Criminal Justice

CHAPTER 1

The Legal System Perspective

continued

PART TWO

An article written by: **Mark Hinkston,** Attorney

Attorney Mark Hinkston was also featured in the CBS 58 story and he has written a very in-depth article on Wisconsin's Castle Doctrine legislation. Wisconsin's law is very similar to other laws on the books of many states so be sure to check your state's law for the exact requirements you need to follow or the protections it provides you in a Self-Defense incident.

[Reprinted from the Wisconsin Lawyer Vol. 85, No. 7, July 2012]

WISCONSIN'S CONCEALED CARRY LAW:

Protecting Persons and Property

Here is an in-depth look at the concealed carry law's provisions, how it applies in various property contexts, and practical ramifications and potential legal issues arising from the law's enactment.

Wisconsin has had a long yet somewhat erratic tradition of gun ownership and use, whether for hunting, sport, or security. The state's early settlers openly carried weapons as tools for sustenance and survival. Conversely, many other people condemned concealed weapons as tools of cowards and impulsive criminals, leading to their ban in Wisconsin in 1872. A year later, Gov. Cadwallader C. Washburn boasted that Wisconsin "was never more free from crime."[1] But the decline would not last. As with the rest of the nation, Wisconsin's social and technological transformation over the ensuing century wrought an explosion in crime.

As a result of the increase in crime, developments in firearms technology, and ubiquitous media images, modern Wisconsinites as a whole tolerate openly displayed weapons far less than did their frontier predecessors. Throughout much of the 19th century, a man could walk in public visibly armed with a holstered firearm and go virtually unnoticed. Doing the same thing today – although legal if done peaceably[2] – will likely invite onlookers' anxiety and law enforcement scrutiny.[3] Until late last year, the combination of fear of crime and fear of public reaction left three unpalatable choices for a Wisconsin resident wishing to enhance self-defense: carry a concealed weapon and risk criminal conviction; openly carry a weapon and scare everyone in sight; or go unarmed into potentially crime-ridden areas.

Ultimately, discomfort over openly carried weapons and recognition of the need for armed self-defense in some contexts led to passage of the Personal Protection Act (2011 Wisconsin Act 35), more commonly known as Wisconsin's Concealed Carry Law (CCL).[4] Passage of the CCL, which took effect Nov. 1, 2011, and was enacted on the premise of "making Wisconsin safer for all responsible, law abiding citizens,"[5] made Wisconsin the 49th state to allow concealed carry (with Illinois the sole prohibiting state).

The CCL allows the carrying of concealed weapons with a state-issued license. In general, it establishes parameters for the licensure and regulation of individuals wishing to carry concealed weapons in the state, dictates where concealed weapons will be prohibited, and lets property and business owners decide whether to allow concealed weapons on their premises. This article 1) highlights the CCL's provisions, 2) discusses concealed carry in various property contexts, and 3) addresses practical ramifications and potential legal issues emanating from the new law's enactment.

Background

Wisconsin enacted its first law against concealed carry on Feb. 14, 1872. It prohibited a person from going "armed with a concealed dirk, dagger, sword, pistol, or pistols, revolver, slung-shot, brass knuckles, or other offensive and dangerous weapon," contained a self-defense exception, and excused individuals who possessed a concealed weapon "with harmless intent."[6] These exceptions, and the specific list of weapons, were redacted in 1878. Thereafter, Wisconsin's law against concealed weapons remained relatively unchanged.[7] From 1955 (when it was codified as Wis. Stat. section 941.23) to 2011 when the CCL was passed, the concealed-carry prohibition provided as follows: "Any person except a peace officer who goes armed with a concealed and dangerous weapon is guilty of a Class A misdemeanor." [*Editor's Note:* For more background information, please see "A Brief History of Concealed Weapons in Wisconsin," available only online with this article at.]

In 1998, Wisconsin voters approved a constitutional amendment (article 1, section 25) giving the people "the right to keep and bear arms for security, defense, hunting, recreation or any other lawful purpose." A debate ensued over whether and to what extent this "fundamental"[8] and "broad constitutional right to keep and bear arms"[9] conflicted with the concealed weapons ban under Wis. Stat. section 941.23, which was seen as "essentially a strict liability offense."[10] There was growing recognition that an absolute ban on "concealed carry" under all circumstances did not suit modern society and that citizens in some contexts (such as those doing business in high-crime areas) should be allowed to carry concealed weapons.[11]

In 2003, in *State v. Hamdan,* the Wisconsin Supreme Court addressed the issue of the viability of Wis. Stat. section 941.23 vis-à-vis the state constitutional right to bear arms. In that case, the court overturned the concealed-weapon conviction of a store owner who kept a firearm on the premises because of prior armed robberies and shootings. (Police officers doing a liquor license check discovered that the owner concealed the gun (normally kept on the counter) on his person while in the process of taking it to the back room for storage.) The supreme court held that the right to keep and bear arms must "permit a person to possess, carry, and sometimes conceal arms to maintain the security of his private residence or privately operated business, and to safely move and store weapons within these premises."[12]

The court noted that without clarification the situation would present a continuing dilemma for law enforcement. It urged "the legislature to thoughtfully examine" Wis. Stat. section 941.23 "and to consider the possibility of a licensing or permit system for persons who have a good reason to carry a concealed weapon."[13] The legislature promptly accepted the invitation. Although two initial measures (in 2003 and 2005) were vetoed and overrides fell short, a third attempt led to the 2011 enactment of the CCL.

The Wisconsin Department of Justice (DOJ) is responsible for oversight and administration of the CCL and issuance of concealed-carry permits. The agency anticipated that it would issue 125,000 permits in the law's first year. It reached the 100,000 mark in less than six months (on April 20, 2012) and expects to easily surpass the projected level of 125,000. This would correlate to just over 2 percent of Wisconsin's population, which is close to the approximate percentage of all U.S. citizens that currently possess concealed-carry licenses.[14]

The Law's Content

The new law is generally an aggregate of an amended carrying-concealed-weapons statute (Wis. Stat. section 941.23), a newly created statute entitled "License to carry a concealed weapon" (Wis. Stat. section 175.60), and an amended trespass-to-land statute (Wis. Stat. section 943.13).

SECTION 941.23, AS AMENDED (Carrying Concealed Weapons)

Although the CCW statute, section 941.23, has been for most of its existence a one-sentence proviso, it has now been extensively broadened, in effect greatly expanding the scope of persons who may lawfully carry a concealed weapon. Now, under the statute, any person "who carries a concealed and dangerous weapon is guilty of a Class A misdemeanor" unless that person is a peace officer, qualified out-of-state law enforcement officer, a former officer, or a concealed carry licensee or out-of-state licensee pursuant to Wis. Stat. section 175.60. (For ease of discussion, in this article "licensee" refers to both resident and nonresident licensees).

Apparently in recognition of the *Hamdan* decision, the statute exempts an individual who carries a concealed and dangerous weapon in his or her own dwelling or place of business or on land that he or she owns, leases, or legally occupies.[15] In all other places where concealed carry is not prohibited, a person must possess a valid license to lawfully carry a concealed weapon.

SECTION 175.60, AS CREATED (License to Carry a Concealed Weapon)

DOJ Rules and Website. The crux of the CCL, newly enacted Wis. Stat. section 175.60, sets forth the general parameters for the issuance and administration of concealed carry licenses.[16] The DOJ has also promulgated proposed rules to implement its responsibilities under the law, namely the issuance of licenses (setting forth the licensing standards and procedures), including verification of applicant credentials and confirmation that the applicant has met training requirements; administration of DOJ-issued licenses; and maintenance of licensing records. The DOJ's website contains information about the new law, including the proposed administrative rules and a frequently-asked-questions section, as well as application forms.[17]

Lexicon and Miscellany. The law does not change basic terminology. To *carry* means "to go armed with," which has been interpreted by Wisconsin courts as meaning that "the weapon was on the defendant's person or that the weapon must have been within the defendant's reach and that the defendant was aware of the presence of the weapon." "Concealed" is not defined under the CCL but generally means that "a weapon is hidden from ordinary observation."[18] *Weapon* under the CCL means a *handgun*, an electric weapon (such as a taser), a knife other than a switchblade, or a billy club. Handgun does not include a machine gun, a short-barreled rifle, or a shotgun.[19]

More History of Concealed Carry in Wisconsin...

If you'd like to learn more about the concealed carry of weapons in Wisconsin, please see "A Brief History of Concealed Weapons in Wisconsin," available with this article online only at **www.wisbar.org/concealedcarry**.

The CCL does not dispense with most preexisting firearms prohibitions. It is still unlawful, under Wis. Stat. section 941.20, to carry a concealed firearm while intoxicated or while unlawfully using controlled substances, point a firearm at another person, intentionally discharge a firearm into a vehicle or building or from a vehicle, or endanger the safety of another person by the negligent operation or handling of a dangerous weapon. And it remains unlawful, under Wis. Stat. section 941.29 and 948.60, for a person who is a felon, a minor, mentally ill, or under an abuse or harassment injunction to possess a firearm, even with a suspended or revoked concealed-carry license.

Although the new law also does not infringe on or significantly limit a person's right to openly carry a firearm, it does clarify that right.[20] Despite the Wisconsin Attorney General's attempt in 2009 (via an advisory memo) to facilitate uniform enforcement of the disorderly-conduct laws in the open-carry context, it was perceived that until the CCL, "open-carry rights were not clearly established under the state or federal constitutions."[21] The CCL amends the disorderly-conduct statutes by requiring "facts and circumstances that indicate a criminal or malicious intent on the part of the person" to support a disorderly-conduct charge, regardless of whether a "firearm is loaded or is concealed or openly carried."[22]

The new law also affects how weapons may lawfully be transported by vehicle. Under prior law, firearms transported in a vehicle had to be encased and unloaded, not within reach, and concealed. Under Wis. Stat. section 167.31, a CCL licensee may carry a concealed weapon, loaded or unloaded, in a vehicle, and a person without a license may place, possess, or transport a handgun in a vehicle without it being unloaded or encased and load a handgun in a vehicle, but the weapon cannot be concealed or hidden and within reach.

"Shall Issue." Wisconsin's new concealed-carry-licensing process, like that of most states, is a *shall issue* process in that officials must issue a license if the applicant satisfies certain minimum requirements (as opposed to a "may issue" process, which affords more discretion to issuing officials). To that end, the DOJ "shall issue" a license to carry a concealed weapon to any individual who is a Wisconsin resident 21 years old or older who completes the specified application process, undergoes required training, is not prohibited by federal or state law from possessing a firearm, and is not prohibited from possessing a dangerous weapon as a condition of release in a criminal case.[23] An applicant must also pass a background check to determine whether he or she is prohibited under federal or state law from possessing a firearm.[24]

Concealed Carry Restrictions

	POSTING	POSTING GROUNDS	PARKING LOT	FIREARMS PROHIBITED BY LAW
Residence (single-family)	**No posting requirement specified - notice may be oral**	**No posting requirement specified - notice may be oral**	**N/A**	**N/A**
Multifamily (condominium/apartment)	**No posting requirement specified - notice may be oral**	**Common areas:** Post at entrances to restricted portion of building & probable access points to restricted grounds	**May not prohibit firearms on grounds used for parking**	
Nonresidential Building (includes nursing homes, community-based residential facilities, residential care apartment complexes, hospices)	**Post signs in prominent place near all entrances where entrant can be reasonably expected to see the sign**	**Post sign in a prominent place near all probable access points where entrant can be reasonably expected to see the sign**	**May not prohibit firearms on grounds used for parking**	**SCHOOLS:** Concealed carry licensees allowed within 1000 feet of school grounds but not on school grounds **TAVERNS:** Concealed carry licensee allowed only if not consuming alcohol on premises
Vacant Land	**To prohibit trespass in general, may notify "No Trespassing" personally (oral or writing) or post sign**	**Post sign in a prominent place near all probable access points where entrant can be reasonably expected to see the sign**	**N/A**	**N/A**
Special Event (event of 3 weeks or less, open to public, with either entrances locked when event is closed or admission fee)	**Post sign in prominent place near all entrances and where entrant can be reasonably expected to see the sign**	**Post sign in prominent place near all entrances and where entrant can be reasonably expected to see the sign**	**May not prohibit firearms in any part of special event building or grounds used as a parking facility**	
State/Local Government Unit	**In any part of a building that is owned, occupied, or controlled by the state or any local governmental unit - post signs in prominent place near all entrances and where entrant can be reasonably expected to see the sign**	**May not prohibit firearms on governmental "grounds or land" (i.e., parks) (unless being used for "Special Event")**	**May not prohibit firearms in parking facilities**	**Open firearms & firearms without concealed-carry license:** prohibited in all governmental buildings. **With concealed-carry license, still prohibited in:** • Police stations • Prisons/jails • Mental health facilities • Courthouses • Airports (beyond security checkpoint)
University/College	**Post signs in prominent place near entrances where entrant can see them**	**May not prohibit firearms on campus grounds (areas outside of buildings)**	**May not prohibit firearms in parking facilities**	

Application, Background Check, and Training. Application forms are available on the DOJ website or, on request, by mail. After receiving the application, the $50 fee, and proof of training, the DOJ conducts a background check and must issue or deny the license within 21 days after receipt of a complete application.[25] A license issued under this section is valid for five years.[26] The DOJ has the authority to revoke or suspend licenses under specified circumstances and has promulgated a rule regarding the denial, suspension, and revocation of licenses.[27]

Applicants must undergo a training regimen. Although the DOJ initially dictated that four hours of training was required, there is no longer a minimum-hour requirement.[28] The DOJ has also prepared a model training curriculum for use by law enforcement agencies and DOJ-certified instructors.

DOJ Database. The DOJ maintains a computerized record listing the names and license information of all licensees. Law enforcement agencies may access or obtain information in the DOJ database only under limited circumstances, and the DOJ may not make database information available to the public "except in the context of a prosecution for an offense in which the person's status as a licensee or holder of a certification card is relevant."[29]

Prohibited Areas and Penalties. Licensees "may carry a concealed weapon anywhere in this state" except 1) a police station, sheriff's office, state patrol station, or the DOJ's division of criminal investigation; 2) a prison, jail, house of correction, or secured correctional facility; 3) any secured portion of a mental health institute; 4) county, state, and federal courthouses (with exceptions for judges, district attorneys, and persons having written judicial authorization); 5) municipal courtrooms when court is in session; and 6) places beyond an airport security checkpoint. (These are hereinafter referred to as "gun-free zones.") However, the concealed-weapon prohibition does not extend to parking facilities affiliated with these locations.[30]

It is generally a crime, under Wis. Stat. section 948.605, for any person to carry (openly or concealed) a firearm in or on the grounds of a school or within 1,000 feet of the grounds. A licensee may possess a firearm within 1,000 feet of school grounds but not in or on school grounds. Under Wis. Stat. section 941.237(3)(cx), a licensee may not carry a concealed weapon in a tavern unless he or she "is not consuming alcohol on the premises."

Penalties for violations of Wis. Stat. section 175.60 range from minor forfeitures for failing to carry a license or report an address change to, for example, a fine of up to $500 or imprisonment for up to 30 days or both for the more serious offense of carrying a concealed weapon in a prohibited area.[31]

SECTION 943.13, AS AMENDED (Trespass to Land)

In addition to the gun-free zones specified by Wis. Stat. section 175.60, certain other areas may be designated as off-limits to weapons. Owners and occupants (including tenants and lessees) may prohibit the carrying of weapons – openly or concealed – on certain property. Wisconsin Statutes section 943.13 ("Trespass to land") permits owners and occupants to prohibit persons from carrying a firearm, concealed or otherwise, in or on property by providing notice (generally a posted sign) that a person may not enter or remain on the property with a firearm. A person may be subject to a Class B forfeiture (a fine not to exceed $1,000) if he or she carries a firearm on the property after being notified not to enter or remain on the property with a firearm or with a specific type of firearm.[32]

Prohibiting Concealed Carry: Posting Guidelines. In places where firearms are prohibited by law (such as in police stations, courthouses, and schools), specific notice need not be posted because entrants are legally presumed to be aware of the prohibition. In all locations where an owner or occupant is allowed to prohibit firearms, the owner or occupant must do so by providing notice of the firearm prohibition. The type of notice depends on the nature of the property and its use.

The nature of the property and the operations thereon as well as the status of the owner will dictate how, and to what extent, an owner of property not in a gun-free zone may restrict (or allow) concealed carry. The discussion below describes the extent to which owners of residential and nonresidential properties (including businesses, government, and colleges and universities) may prohibit concealed carry and the manner of doing so (via signage).

Residential: Oral or Posting Notice. The law does not expressly provide a method that owners, tenants, and occupants of a residence – whether single family or non single family (such as condominiums or apartment complexes) – must use to give notice. Presumably, they may do so either orally or with a sign.[33]

Nonresidential: Posting. In all other scenarios (such as businesses, governmental buildings, and college and university buildings, including dorms), to prohibit weapons a sign of at least 5 by 7 inches must be posted in a "prominent place" near generally specified areas where entrants "can be reasonably expected to see the sign." The statute mandates no specific language or color for the sign, other than it must reference the "restriction imposed" (not to enter, or remain on, the premises with a firearm or a particular type of firearm).[34]

The accompanying table illustrates the various posting requirements, contained in Wis. Stat. section 943.13(2). Rules of thumb are the following: 1) for *buildings* where posting is desired (restricted portions of condominiums and apartment complexes, nonresidential buildings, local and state governmental buildings, and universities and colleges), signs should be placed in a prominent and reasonably visible place near all entrances; 2) for *grounds*, such as condominium and apartment common areas and land surrounding nonresidential structures, signs should be placed near all probable access points to the grounds or land to which the restriction applies; and 3) for a *special event*, which is an event, open to the public, scheduled to last no more than three weeks and having either designated entrances to and from the event that are locked at closing or requiring an admission, signs should be posted near all entrances.

May Not Prohibit: Public and Campus "Grounds"; Parking Facilities. There are several areas where, by law, one may not prohibit weapons, openly carried or concealed. For example, colleges and universities may not prohibit weapons on campus grounds (areas outside buildings), and governmental units may not prohibit weapons on public "grounds or land" (such as county parks, but not buildings or shelters in those parks). Also, "if a firearm is in a vehicle driven or parked in the parking facility," a firearms prohibition will not extend "to any part of a building, grounds, or land used as a parking facility."[35]

Three Special Contexts: Employers, Municipalities, and Tenancies

Employers. The new law provides certain guidelines and restrictions for employers, regardless of size. An employer may generally prohibit an employee who has a valid concealed-carry license from carrying a concealed weapon or a particular type of concealed weapon in the course of his or her employment. However, an employer may not, as a condition of employment, prohibit a licensee from carrying or storing in the licensee's own motor vehicle a concealed weapon, a particular type of concealed weapon, or ammunition, even if the motor vehicle is used in the course of employment or driven or parked on the employer's property. However, an employer may ban concealed weapons from employer-owned vehicles (and from vehicles owned by persons not possessing a valid concealed-carry license).[36]

Municipalities. Since the new law's enactment, many Wisconsin municipalities have enacted ordinances or resolutions to prohibit weapons in certain portions of governmental buildings (where weapons are already not prohibited by law). As for state buildings, concealed carry is allowed in most state facilities, with some exceptions.[37] (The State Assembly even voted to allow concealed carry on its floor and in its galleries; at least one legislator has publicly announced that he has a concealed-carry license and periodically carries a concealed weapon in the Assembly).[38]

Municipalities are barred, by Wis. Stat. section 66.0409(2), from adopting ordinances or resolutions regulating concealed carry more stringently than does the CCL. Thus, because the applicable state statute mandates that firearms may not be prohibited on municipal property and grounds (such as parks) or in parking facilities, a municipal ordinance prohibiting firearms in such areas would presumably be invalid and unenforceable.

Tenancies. Businesses often lease the space where they conduct their business. Rental property is generally comprised of three areas: the leased area, a common area, and a parking lot. It is clear that property owners (in this case, that is, landlords) may determine whether and to what extent they will prohibit or allow concealed weapons in the common areas. Neither the landlord nor the tenant may prohibit firearms in parking areas. As for the leased space, one presumes that the tenant, and not the landlord, would have the decision whether to prohibit concealed weapons as to the leased space (residential or commercial), in the absence of a provision in the lease providing otherwise.

The viability of lease provisions under which a tenant abdicates to the landlord authority to decide whether to allow or prohibit firearms on the leased premises is not absolutely clear under the new law. In some states, it is apparent that a tenant can give up the right to possess firearms in his or her leased premises.[39] Wisconsin law does not necessarily reject such a proposition. However, a tenant could challenge such a lease provision by alleging, for example, that it conflicts with Wisconsin's broad constitutional right to keep and bear arms or the legislature's proclamation that concealed carry is not illegal in one's dwelling, business, or on land that "he or she owns, leases, or legally occupies."

Illustrations: Proprietors, Employers, Municipalities

Under the CCL, a person who does not prohibit individuals from carrying concealed weapons on property the person owns or occupies is "immune from any liability arising from" such decision. Employers that do not prohibit employees from carrying concealed weapons are also afforded immunity "from any liability arising from" such decision.[40] The question arises: Is the purported immunity grant a truly protective incentive or a mere illusion?[41] A series of illustrations in three contexts (businesses, places of employment, and municipalities) may assist in examining that question.

Proprietors: Foresee Ability Is Key. *Illustration:* A store owner posts a "No Guns Allowed" sign. The sign is smaller than the requisite 5- by 7-inch size and is not easily seen by entrants. Store employees are not allowed to carry concealed weapons, but the owner keeps a handgun hidden near the front register in case of emergency. An armed assailant enters the store, points a gun at the cashier, and demands money. Customer A tries to thwart the attack by pulling out a concealed handgun and shooting at the assailant, who is struggling with the cashier for control of the firearm kept near the register. Customer A inadvertently shoots the cashier, who has wrestled the front-register gun away from the assailant. When the mortally wounded cashier hits the ground, his gun fires, wounding Customer B. Customer B sues the store owner and Customer A.

Assume that the plaintiff (Customer B) first predicates liability on a contention that the lack of immunity under the CCL automatically imposes liability. This is a nonstarter. Although one can assume that the immunity proviso was included as an enticement to promote concealed carry, an absence of immunity for persons who prohibit concealed weapons should not be equated with *ipso facto* liability if there is a shooting incident on the premises. There is no basis in the law's content or history (or under existing common law) for such an interpretation. In such cases, a plaintiff must still allege and prove a recognized and viable legal claim against a defendant.

Assume that, alternatively, the plaintiff contends that the owner was negligent in 1) prohibiting concealed weapons, 2) improperly posting a "No Guns Allowed" sign, and 3) not implementing adequate safety precautions in view of the neighborhood and the history of criminal activity at the store. The first two of these bases are weak. Although it can be argued that by prohibiting concealed weapons, the owner has deprived licensees on the premises the opportunity to defend themselves and thus has assumed responsibility,[42] this seems to be a fairly absurd position given that the legislature obviously gave owners a choice of whether to allow or prohibit concealed carry. Moreover, the mere posting of a sign does not make it foreseeable that a criminal will enter the premises on a certain day and create havoc.[43]

As to the second basis, that the "No Guns Allowed" sign is ineffective (too small and not easily seen), this too would likely fail since it is highly unlikely that one could prove that had a proper sign been properly posted, the assailant would never have targeted the store. Individuals bent on crime will likely be undeterred by a sign (and some may even be attracted by such a sign, believing that no one on the premises will be armed).[44]

These bases are moored by a "disarmed victim" paradigm, which assumes that the victim, if armed, certainly could have thwarted the attack or shooting. However, in *Jones v. Tokhi*, the Wisconsin Court of Appeals noted that shooting or attempting to disarm an attacker is far easier said than done: "When victims are facing the barrel of a gun and listening to threats to shoot them, it is difficult to know what they should do. Actions that seem prudent and prove successful under one set of circumstances may prove disastrous under others."[45] In view of this uncertainty when a victim faces a gun barrel, it is unlikely that a court could ever rule as a matter of law that a proprietor should be held liable to a victim merely because the proprietor prohibited concealed weapons on the premises.

The highest likelihood of success comes with the third basis: that the history and location of the store mandated extra precautions. Even so, "liability for criminal acts" cases against business proprietors "are difficult cases which will present our trial courts with many matters of complex factual proof."[46] A proprietor "is not required to guarantee the safety of patrons against injuries inflicted by other patrons on the premises."[47] To impose liability, foresee ability is key: liability will not be imposed unless the danger presented was foreseeable and could have been prevented or stopped within time. Because shootings often occur in a flash and without warning, in many such circumstances it will not be easy to impose liability on a proprietor.[48]

Factors that a court might evaluate to determine whether a particular danger was foreseeable include the nature of the business, industry standards, the community's crime rate, and the number of prior similar incidents or police calls to the premises.[49] In the absence of any prior criminal incidents, the absence of security does not constitute a breach of a proprietor's duty to protect patrons.[50] If there is an attack, a plaintiff must show that the proprietor had knowledge of the perpetrator's "violent propensities" and that the defendant could have undertaken action in sufficient time to stop or control the perpetrator.[51]

As for liability against Customer A, the errant-shooting "Good Samaritan," the CCL does not expressly afford immunity. However, liability would likely have to hinge on proof that the customer knew that guns were not allowed (communicated via a sign, albeit small) but carried one in anyway, again a daunting proposition.

Employer and Employee Liability. *Illustration:* A 5- by 7-inch "No Guns Allowed" sign is clearly visible to all store entrants. An armed assailant comes to the store looking for his ex-wife, who works there. Employees are prohibited from having concealed weapons on the premises. The assailant confronts the cashier, threatening to shoot him, after the cashier tells him that the ex-wife is not at the store. Hearing the chaos, an employee with a concealed-carry license reaches into his jacket, removes his handgun from its holster, and starts shooting at the assailant. He misses the assailant and accidentally shoots the cashier and a customer instead. The assailant escapes. He had gone to the store to shoot his ex-wife. Not finding her there, he goes to her home and fatally shoots her. (He received her unlisted address via a phone call to her employer impersonating a loan officer doing a credit check.) The injured cashier, injured customer, and estate of the slain ex-wife bring suit.

Employee's (Cashier's) Claim against Employer. Employers do not have a general duty to protect their employees from criminal acts.[52] Employees shot at work by coworkers or third parties will be entitled to worker's compensation coverage (even in situations in which the shooting resulted from an intentional act without a purely personal connection to the employee victim), regardless of whether the employer allowed or prohibited concealed weapons.[53] Moreover, under Wisconsin's safe-place statute, Wis. Stat. section 101.11(1), every employer is required to furnish both "safe employment" and a "safe place of employment." Although the court of appeals has noted that "[p]rotection of employees from injury during an attempted crime by a third-party is part of the employer's duty to provide safe employment," there has been little elaboration on what efforts will satisfy this duty.[54]

Employee's (Ex-wife's) Claim against Employer. When conditions of liability for worker's compensation are satisfied, the exclusive remedy provision of the Worker's Compensation Act (WCA) applies, thereby precluding an injured employee from maintaining a negligence action against his or her employer or a coworker. In a true-life situation similar to that above, in which the injury was caused by the employer's "unwitting disclosure" of "information to a private individual" (the employee's "abusive former husband"), the Wisconsin Supreme Court held that the circumstance was an accident compensable under the WCA.[55]

Customer's Claim against Owner (Employer). Under certain circumstances, employers can be subject to liability for the tortuous or criminal acts of employees committed within the scope of employment.[56] (As with "proprietor liability" cases, the liability bar is high.) In cases involving a shooting injury inflicted by an employee who is a concealed-carry licensee, there will be a two-fold analysis: 1) was the employee acting within the scope of his or her employment,[57] and 2) is the employer immune. (In other words, does the employer's potential liability arise from his or her decision to not prohibit licensed concealed carry on the premises?)[58]

The safe-place statute "provides that it is an employer's duty to provide safe employment, premises and equipment for the protection" of employees and frequenters.[59] But "the safe-place statute does not make the employer an insurer of the safety of a frequenter on the premises" and, therefore, it "*deals with unsafe conditions* of the employer's premises and not with negligent or inadvertent acts of employees or activities conducted on the premises."[60] Therefore, a safe-place negligence claim premised on a failure to timely act in the face of an unannounced and unforeseen shooting will likely fail.

Creative plaintiffs could, in situations such as those in the examples, turn to other bases to skirt the employer immunity, primarily by asserting that the liability arises out of something other than the decision to not prohibit concealed weapons. For example, a plaintiff could focus on the word "decision" and contend that allowing concealed carry by default (for example, not posting signs because of unawareness of the law) is not really a decision per se and thus does not afford immunity.

Situations might also arise in which plaintiffs could attempt to avoid the immunity protection by asserting other claims not "arising from" a concealed-carry decision:

1) If a concealed-carry licensee employee with a troubled past or a history of violence inflicts injury through shooting, plaintiffs will likely premise claims on negligent hiring, supervision, and training.

2) Employers are generally counseled to draft workplace weapons policies if they intend to allow firearms on the premises, and under some circumstances they will implement certain safety or security devices or protocol. Injured third parties could argue that liability should be premised on the failure to strictly enforce such weapons policies (for example, if an employee is not disciplined for continuing violations).[61]

3) An employer that installs security equipment, such as metal detectors or surveillance equipment, has in doing so assumed a duty to act with greater care than otherwise would be imposed. If it fails to follow through by properly and consistently using such equipment and training the personnel in charge of running it, liability might be found to arise.

Plaintiffs might also try to premise liability on a failure to provide a safe workplace under 29 U.S.C. § 654(a)(1), the Occupational Safety and Health Administration's (OSHA's) "general duty clause," which provides that "[e]ach employer shall furnish to each of [its] employees employment and a place of employment which are free from recognized hazards that are causing or likely to cause death or serious physical harm to its employees." But it is unlikely that an employer's allowance of concealed weapons, without more, would invite OSHA oversight, especially because OSHA has not promulgated a specific rule banning weapons in the workplace, and courts have held that the general duty clause does not preempt state gun laws.[62] Moreover, the Wisconsin Court of Appeals has also held that the clause is "not a safety law intended to be the basis for imposing tort liability."[63]

Municipality: Failure to Protect. *Illustration:* The police were summoned to a woman's home via 911 just a few minutes before she was shot by her ex-husband. During the couple's 10-year marriage, law enforcement had been summoned to the house twice.

Does the woman's estate have a claim against the municipality? No. "[I]t is well established that public entities generally are not liable for failing to protect individuals against crime."[64] Thus, law enforcement personnel will generally be immune from liability to shooting victims in most cases involving an alleged "failure to protect the victim" from a third party's act (shooting). The fact that persons and entities that do not prohibit concealed carry are granted immunity as to such decision would not emasculate such sovereign immunity in the concealed-carry context.[65]

Under most circumstances involving shootings, it is likely that municipalities will have the benefit of sovereign immunity. Wisconsin Statutes section 893.80(4) grants to municipalities and their officials and employees immunity from liability for their legislative and quasi-legislative functions, which are generally acts involving "the exercise of discretion and judgment." Decisions whether to prohibit the public and municipal employees from carrying concealed weapons in a municipal building would obviously be categorized as part of the discretionary (not ministerial) function. Thus, immunity under section 893.80(4) will generally protect municipalities that choose to prohibit invitees or employees from carrying concealed weapons on the premises or in the course of their employment.

Shootings in public buildings do not occur frequently, and rarely is the governmental entity held liable for the consequent injuries. Plaintiffs generally are unable to premise liability on an entity's decisions as to adoption and implementation of security plans or a decision to forego having visitors go through monitoring devices (metal detectors) upon entry.[66]

Conclusion

Due to its breadth, the CCL will affect virtually all people in Wisconsin, regardless of their viewpoint on, or experience with, weapons. Even if one does not get a concealed-carry license, he or she may know someone who does, will (likely unknowingly) interact with licensees in public (such as in stores or at entertainment venues), and will frequent businesses that have chosen to prohibit or allow concealed weapons on the premises. In short, along with the law's impact on concealed-carry licensees, it will affect property and business owners, their customers and invitees, and employers and employees.

Gun rights advocates tout Wisconsin's new concealed-carry law as widespread recognition of a long-deserved exercise of the state constitutional right to bear arms, which they believe will inevitably decrease crime. Gun control advocates stress the danger of arming tens of thousands of new licensees and emboldening them with other legislative protections against liability. This article has not taken sides or challenged any beliefs on the subject, other than to neutrally note that as of now, and as portended by the experience in the 48 preceding states, Wisconsin has been transformed into neither the Wild West (gun opponents' fear) nor a crime-free utopia (gun proponents' hope). There has been no demonstrable resulting uptick in violent gun-related crime by trigger-happy gun-owning neophytes. Conversely, passage of the law has not resulted in a significant dip in crime as a result of criminals being rendered gun shy by previously vulnerable citizens who now lawfully (and secretly) pack heat.

The new CCL may present some initial perplexity in implementation and interpretation. As with much new socially significant legislation, many of the currently opaque liability issues will ultimately need to be worked out through judicial consideration and possible legislative supplementation. Unfortunately, most appellate cases considering liability under the new law will inherently present a precipitating incident involving the negligent or intentional discharge of a firearm, leading to injury or death. In view of this reality, this author for one does not wish to become well-versed in real-world concealed-carry liability law, hopes that there are no test cases, and will gladly allow his intellectual curiosity to be piqued solely via insight and illumination by legal commentators, the State Attorney General, and the legislature in due course as it sees fit. In the meantime, one suspects that the many potential liability questions can also keep Wisconsin tort professors supplied with a multitude of examination scenarios for years to come.

Endnotes

[1] Message of Cadwallader C. Washburn, Governor of Wisconsin, Delivered at the Twenty-sixth Annual Session of the Legislature of the State of Wisconsin, Assembled in Joint Convention, Jan. 9, 1873, p. 16.

[2] *See* Advisory Memorandum from Wis. Atty. Gen. J.B. Van Hollen (April 20, 2009) ("The Wisconsin Department of Justice (the Department) believes that the mere open carrying of a firearm by a person, absent additional facts and circumstances, should not result in a disorderly conduct charge from a prosecutor").

[3] *Gonzalez v. Village of W. Milwaukee*, No. 09-CV-384, slip op. at 6 (E.D. Wis. May 11, 2010) ("No reasonable person would dispute that walking into a retail store openly carrying a firearm is highly disruptive conduct which is virtually certain to create a disturbance").

[4] The Department of Justice (DOJ) refers to the new law as the "Carrying a Concealed Weapon Law," with the acronym "CCW." Because Wisconsin appellate courts, including the supreme court, have referred to the criminal statute prohibiting concealed weapons (Wis. Stat. § 941.23) as the "CCW law" or "CCW statute," so as to not conflict with those decisions the author herein uses the acronym "CCL" to refer to the new law allowing concealed carry with a permit.

Two other Wisconsin laws that went into effect in late 2011, ostensibly to increase self-protection, are the subject of a future article: the so-called castle doctrine law

(2011 Wis. Act 94), which creates a presumption of civil and criminal immunity for persons who use force in response to the unlawful and forcible entry into a dwelling, motor vehicle, or business; and the trespasser liability law (2011 Wis. Act 93), which generally provides that private landowners owe no duty of care to a trespasser on their property and may not be found liable for an act or omission relating to a condition on the property causing injury or death to a trespasser.

[5] Jason Stein, *Walker signs concealed-carry measure into law,* Milw. J. Sentinel, July 8, 2011.

[6] § 1, ch. 7, Laws of 1872. "...[S]o going armed shall not be deemed a violation of this act whenever it shall be made to appear that such person had reasonable cause to fear an assault or other injury or violence to his person, or to his family or property, or to any person under his immediate care or custody, or entitled to his protection or assistance...."

[7] After the redaction, the statute read: "Any person who shall go armed with any concealed and dangerous weapon, shall be punished by imprisonment in the county jail not more than six months, or by fine not exceeding one hundred dollars; provided, this section shall not apply to any policeman or officer authorized to serve process." Wis. Stat. § 4397 (1878).

[8] *State v. Cole,* 2003 WI 112, ¶ 21, 264 Wis. 2d 520, 665 N.W.2d 328.

[9] *State v. Hamdan,* 2003 WI 113, ¶ 103, 264 Wis. 2d 433, 665 N.W.2d 785 (Crooks, J., concurring/dissenting).

[10] *Id.* ¶ 48. *See also Gonzalez,* 671 F.3d at 657 ("Before its sweeping modification in 2011, the concealed-weapon statute was in significant tension with the newly adopted constitutional right").

[11] Examples include those "making nighttime bank deposits after closing their stores; seeking protection from serious, threatened attack; [or] traveling to hunt or target shoot without awareness of the legal manner of transporting weapons." *Epstein v. Benson,* 2000 WI App 195, ¶ 44, 238 Wis. 2d 717, 617 N.W.2d 224.

[12] 2003 WI 113, ¶ ¶ 48, 103, 264 Wis. 2d 433.

[13] Id. ¶ 85.

[14] Patrick Marley, *Wisconsin issues 100,000th concealed-weapon permit,* Milw. J. Sentinel, April 20, 2012; Mike Stuckey, *Record numbers licensed to pack heat,* June 24, 2010, http://tinyurl.com/7ob6qjh (estimating at 6 million the number of concealed-carry permit holders nationwide).

[15] Wis. Stat. §§ 941.23(2)(e), 941.295(2)(d)2.

[16] The DOJ "may not impose conditions, limitations, or requirements that are not expressly provided for" in Wis. Stat. section 175.60 "on the issuance, scope, effect, or content of a license." Wis. Stat. § 175.60(2)(b).

[17] www.doj.state.wi.us/dles/cib/ConcealedCarry/ConcealedCarry.asp.

[18] *State v. Asfoor,* 75 Wis. 2d 411, 433-34, 249 N.W.2d 529 (1977).

[19] Wis. Stat. § 175.60(1)(bm), (j).

[20] *See* Wis. Stat. § 175.60(2)(c) (unless expressly stated otherwise, it "does not limit an individual's right to carry a firearm that is not concealed").

[21] *Gonzalez v. Village of W. Milwaukee,* 671 F.3d 649, 660 (7th Cir. 2012).

[22] Wis. Stat. §§ 66.0409(6), 947.01(2).

[23] Wis. Stat. § 175.60(2), (3).

[24] Wis. Stat. § 175.60(9g).

[25] Wis. Stat. § 175.60(4), (5), (5b), (7), (9), (9g).

[26] Wis. Stat. § 175.60(15)(a).

[27] Wis. Stat. § 175.60(14).

[28] Wis. Stat. § 175.60(4).

[29] Wis. Stat. § 175.60(12), (12g).

[30] Wis. Stat. § 175.60(16).

[31] Wis. Stat. § 175.60(17).

[32] Wis. Stat. § 943.13(1m)(c), (2)(bm).

[33] Wis. Stat. § 943.13(2)(am).

[34] Wis. Stat. § 943.13(2)(bm).

[35] Wis. Stat. § 943.13(1m)(c)2.

[36] Wis. Stat. § 175.60(15m).

[37] Mike Johnson & Larry Sandler, *Some cities act to ban guns from government buildings,* Milw. J. Sentinel, Aug. 20, 2011; Jason Stein, Most state buildings get OK for guns, Milw. J. Sentinel, Oct. 28, 2011.

[38] Associated Press, *GOP lawmaker packing gun on Assembly floor,* Milw. J. Sentinel, Feb. 3, 2012.

[39] *See, e.g.,* Op. Tenn. Att'y Gen. 09-170 (Oct. 26, 2009) ("A landlord can prohibit tenants, including those who hold handgun carry permits, from possessing firearms within the leased premises").

[40] Wis. Stat. § 175.60(21)(b), (c).

[41] In a Nov. 8, 2011, letter, Wisconsin state senators Tim Cullen and Jon Erpenbach requested a legal opinion from attorney general J.B. Van Hollen on the issue of the extent to which a person or entity that bans concealed carry may be liable, stating that the new law's immunity provisions "are counterintuitive and illogical, not to mention outrageous" in that they afford immunity to those who allow concealed weapons. They contend that those who allow weapons on their premises "should have to take extra precautions to ensure the safety of people on the premises."

[42] *See* A. Nicole Hartley, *Business Owner Liability and Concealed Weapons Legislation: A Call for Legislative Guidance for Pennsylvania Business Owners*, 108 Penn. St. L. Rev. 637, 644 (2003).

[43] *See* Texas Atty. Gen. Op. DM-363 (Aug. 30, 1995).

[44] See Thomas E.J. "Tobie" Hazard, *In the Crosshairs: Colorado's New Gun Laws*, 33 Colo. Law. 1, 17 (2004).

[45] 193 Wis. 2d 514, 522, 535 N.W.2d 46 (Ct. App. 1995) (in a case in which the plaintiff, a high school basketball star, was shot while in a restaurant parking lot at 1:45 a.m., reversing circuit court's postverdict decision that the plaintiff's attempt to disarm the gunman constituted negligence that exceeded the defendants' negligence as a matter of law, rebuffing defendants' argument that plaintiff knew that the likelihood of being shot would increase if he tried to disarm his attacker).

[46] *Peters v. Holiday Inns Inc.*, 89 Wis. 2d 115, 129, 278 N.W.2d 208 (1979).

[47] Wis. JI-Civil 8045 ("Duty of a Proprietor of a Place of Business to Protect a Patron From Injury Caused By Act of Third Person"). *See Hawkes v. Bagain*, No. 03-0754-FT, ¶ 6 (Wis. Ct. App. Sept. 9, 2003) (citing *Weihert v. Piccione*, 273 Wis. 448, 456, 78 N.W.2d 757 (1956)) ("The degree of care required by employees fluctuates with the facts and circumstances of each particular case").

[48] In Wisconsin, a proprietor is subject to liability for injury caused by a third party's criminal act "if the proprietor by the exercise of reasonable care could have discovered that such acts were being done or were about to be done, and could have protected the members of the public by controlling the conduct of the third persons, or by giving a warning adequate to enable them to avoid harm." *Weihert*, 273 Wis. 448 (holding, in case in which restaurant patron was beaten and injured when altercation broke out between customers, owner was not liable because owner could not have discovered that fight was about to occur or warned plaintiffs that any altercation might happen).

[49] *Peters*, 89 Wis. 2d at 124.

[50] *Kolstad v. White Birch Inn LLC*, No. 2007AP002970 (Wis. Ct. App. Sept. 16, 2008).

[51] *Griffin v. V & J Foods Inc.*, No. 95-1335-FT (Wis. Ct. App. Jan. 16, 1996) (holding that fast food restaurant was not liable for injuries to plaintiff shot while waiting in drive-through lane because there was no evidence that the staff had notice or knowledge of shooter's "violent propensities" and no liability for failure to summon police because evidence showed that even if police had been called, they could not have intervened in time).

[52] *Dupont v. Aavid Thermal Tech.*, 798 A.2d 587 (N.H. 2002).

[53] *Weiss v. City of Milwaukee*, 208 Wis. 2d 95, 559 N.W.2d 588 (1997).

[54] *Naaj v. Aetna Ins. Co.*, 218 Wis. 2d 121, 579 N.W.2d 815 (Ct. App. 1998).

[55] *Weiss*, 208 Wis. 2d 95.

[56] *Pamperin v. Trinity Mem'l Hosp.*, 144 Wis. 2d 188, 198, 423 N.W.2d 848 (1988).

[57] See Wis. JI-Civil 4035 ("Servant: Scope of Employment").

[58] It is not clear who has the burden of proof on this issue (whether the employer must prove that its decision and alleged liability are connected or whether the plaintiff must prove that something other than the decision to allow licensed concealed weapons is the basis for liability). *But see Kimps v. Hill*, 200 Wis. 2d 1, 18-19, 546 N.W.2d 151 (1996) ("it should be noted that Hill does not carry a burden to demonstrate that he is entitled to immunity; on the contrary, the general rule for state employees is immunity and an exception must be demonstrated in order for this rule not to apply").

[59] *Stefanovich v. Iowa Nat'l Mut. Ins. Co.*, 86 Wis. 2d 161, 166, 271 N.W.2d 867 (1978).

[60] *Montey v. Steve's on Bluemound*, No. 99-1612 (Wis. Ct. App. Sept. 19, 2000).

[61] Note, *Weapons In the Workplace: The Effect of Tennessee's Concealed Weapons Statute on Employer Liability*, 28 U. Memphis L. Rev. 281 (1997).

[62] *See, e.g., Florida Retail Fed'n v. Atty. Gen. of Fl.*, 576 F. Supp. 2d 1281, 1298 (N.D. Fla. 2008).

[63] *Taft v. Derricks*, 2000 WI App 103, ¶ 29, 235 Wis. 2d 22, 613 N.W.2d 190.

[64] Zelig v. County of Los Angeles, 27 Cal. 4th 1112, 1126, 45 P.3d 1171 (2002). *See also* District of Columbia v. Harris, 770 A.2d 82, 87 (D.C. 2001).

[65] See Claire Silverman, League of Wisconsin Municipalities, December 2011 Comment, Oct. 31, 2011, Frequent Questions Arising under Wisconsin's Concealed Carry Law, *available at* www.lwm-info.org.

[66] *See, e.g., Sczyrek v. County of Essex*, 324 N.J. Super. 235, 241-42, 735 A.2d 33 (1999) ("Here, the decision of the Essex County authorities respecting adoption of a security plan, the decision as to how that plan should operate, and the question of whether and to what extent employees and others should be required to pass through monitoring devices, epitomizes the policy or political decisions entrusted to governmental officials, with which judges and juries should not interfere. They are decisions that reside with the public entity,..."); Zelig, 27 Cal. 4th at 1130 ("To the extent the complaint relies on the policy decisions of unnamed public officers and employees with regard to the nature and degree of security that should be utilized in the courthouse to protect all of its users – for example, decisions regarding the posting of signs or the installation and operation of metal detectors – such conduct would not give rise to liability on the part of these persons").

Reprinted from the Wisconsin Lawyer Vol. 85, No. 7, July 2012

http://www.wisbar.org/AM/Template.cfm?Section=business_law_section&CONTENTID=112144&TEMPLATE=/cm/contentdisplay.cfm

Mark R. Hinkston

Creighton 1988 cum laude
Practices law at Hinkston Law Office S.C.
and is of counsel to Knuteson, Powers & Quinn S.C., Racine.

His practice is primarily devoted to business and construction litigation.

Mark can be reached at mhinkston@sbcglobal.net.

CHAPTER 2

THE preferred program for Concealed Carry and Self Defense

CCW SAFE / CIVIL SUIT COVERAGE COMBINATION

Offered exclusively through Affordable Insurance Solutions LLC
Get a quote by calling: **608-663-9800**
Or visit **www.ConcealedCarryInsurance.com**

CCW SAFE

Legal fee Protection for Criminal Defense relating to a Self-Defense shooting:

So what the heck IS CCW Safe? It is NOT insurance...which in this case is even BETTER because there are no limits to the amount of benefits you can receive for a criminal defense in a Self-Defense incident.

Here's how it works...you become a member by paying an annual fee currently at $99.00 per year. This membership will pay all of your criminal defense legal fees directly for you on your behalf (not a reimbursement of fees you pay out of pocket) right from the start if you happen to be involved in a Self-Defense shooting as long as you are carrying a weapon legally with a Concealed Carry License.

Many CCW Licensees have permits or licenses for multiple states like I do (Wisconsin and Utah) and the CCW Safe membership will cover you anywhere you are carrying a weapon legally with your license. For example, if I am carrying while at my in-laws in Iowa or Minnesota I am legal because that falls under my Utah permit. My CCW Safe membership would provide Legal Fee Protection for me in those states.

Now, if I was stupid enough to be carrying a weapon while at my relatives in Illinois and I was involved in a Self-Defense incident, I would NOT have any legal fee protection since I do not have a Concealed Carry license in that state and I would be carrying a weapon illegally.

There is no limit to the amount of benefit your membership would give you for your legal defense...if it cost $5,000 they pay the $5,000...if it costs $250,000 they'd pay the $250,000 (think George Zimmerman here!). As long as the shooting can be claimed as Self-Defense they will be by your side.

So what does that mean exactly?

As long as you don't walk up to someone, pull out your gun and shoot them in a criminal manner (murder, etc.) they will stand by you and defend you in a court of law.

Take this scenario for example that I will use to show how and why you would want and need protection:

You are carrying your weapon concealed and you stop to get gas and a cup of coffee on the way to work. While inside a gunman rushes in and not seeing you, points his gun at the cashier and asks for money...as you are backing away slowly to get to a safer position he sees you, swings the gun on you, you feel threatened and you shoot the guy...dead or not it is most-likely Self-Defense right?

Most-likely...but that doesn't mean you are automatically cleared of wrongdoing even if there are video surveillance cameras that caught the whole thing on tape. You will still need to give your statement to the police and you will still need to meet with the District Attorney's office to make sure you are cleared of any criminal wrongdoing...and you are definitely going to want to have an Attorney represent you during this process!

Your Attorney will help you navigate the legal system in the shortest time possible to get you cleared but that is going to cost money...and as a CCW Safe member they will pay for your Attorney for you no matter how long it takes or how much it costs!

Remember earlier in the book Attorney Paul Bucher said that fees for representation in this type of clear-cut incident can be as much as $5,000... as a CCW Safe member you don't have to pay anything out of pocket – you just call the 24-hour Toll Free Hotline they provide members, inform them of your circumstances and they will take it from there.

Many people ask if CCW Safe will provide the Attorney for you or if you can have your own Attorney represent you. As a CCW Safe member they will pay legal fees for an Attorney they provide and you will want to confirm when you sign up if they will pay for an attorney you specifically request to represent you. If they will not don't worry because they will find you an Attorney who is knowledgeable with the 2nd Amendment and Self-Defense.

Everyone should have the name and phone number of a Criminal Defense Attorney in the event they are involved in a Self-Defense incident but as a CCW Safe member it isn't necessary as long as you have the 24hr hotline number with you.

But what happens if you are travelling out of state?

If you are in unfamiliar territory you would call the 24-hour hotline and tell them what happened, you need legal representation and the CCW Safe team will get you set up with an Attorney and they will pay them for your defense costs.

Many people ask what exactly does CCW Safe pay for in regards to your legal defense...they will pay for your Attorney Fees, expert witnesses and any other costs necessary to defend you in a court of law should it go to trial. Again, there is no limit to the amount they will pay on your behalf...the question is:

Do you want to pay for these things out of your own pocket???

My guess is not really...so at $99 per year the CCW Safe membership is a NO BRAINER!

To get your CCW Safe membership please visit www.CCWSafe.com

The following is taken from the CCW Safe website:

If you are involved in a shooting, or a critical self defense incident, our action plan begins as soon as you make notice to CCW Safe. The following steps will guide you through the process.

Notification

Immediately upon being involved in a critical self defense incident, you will need to notify CCW Safe. First, notify 911 that you are a victim and were forced to defend yourself. Request help and medical support. Next, notify CCW Safe by calling the 24 hour emergency number on your membership card. You will talk to an attorney who will give you guidance on your next action. You will be instructed to give a very basic statement. This statement should include your name, personal information, the fact that you are a victim and were forced to defend yourself, identifying the suspect, any witnesses, and present your CCW permit and CCW Safe membership card. You will be instructed to advise authorities that you have legal representation and that you would like to give a full statement in the presence of your attorney. CCW Safe attorneys may initiate an investigative response team to begin investigation on your incident.

Official Interview

CCW Safe attorneys will attempt to secure a 24 – 48 hour window before any statement is given. This is based on the fact that all parties involved will want the most accurate account of the incident. Once that interview is scheduled, you may give an official statement after consultation with your attorney. You will be advised not to talk to anyone, not even your family and friends about the incident until the official interview is complete. Even after this interview, you will be advised to keep strict discretion about any conversation regarding the incident until the decision is made by the District Attorney or States Attorney on whether any charges will be filed. Any media requests for interviews should be directed to your legal counsel.

Determination Phase

There will be a period of time, ranging from days to weeks that will determine if any criminal charges will be filed. In the case of civil or administrative action, this period of time may be much longer, possibly up to a year or two. During this time, CCW Safe will work with our defense panel attorneys that have been assigned to you to protect the privilege of all investigative reports, interview and other reports necessary to prepare for the "next fight" if needed.

Trial Preparation

It is always possible that civil action and/or criminal charges could be filed. In a civil case (one where someone sues you for causing them an injury based on negligence) there is a long period called discovery. This is the mechanism that all parties have to learn about what evidence there is and what evidence they intend to put on at the time of trial. This is an incredibly costly process of meetings with witnesses, experts, deposition testimony, etc. This all has to be done in advance of a trial. In a criminal charge, there is no discovery phase. There are no depositions. But, there are witness meetings in an attempt to prepare the best possible defense. CCW Safe will provide the lawyers for our members at no cost to the member. This is a savings of tens of thousands of dollars.

Defense Phase

The defense phase is the actual trial process. Again, this can last a long time and can be a very stressful time, perhaps the most stressful time of your entire life. CCW Safe will provide representation throughout the trial process, and even into retrials or appeals if necessary. And remember, no additional fees are charged to the member for this.

To get your CCW Safe membership please visit www.CCWSafe.com

OTHER LEGAL FEE MEMBERSHIPS AVAILABLE

(that in my opinion are inferior to CCW Safe)

Patriot Legal

Patriot Legal is very similar to CCW Safe and they actually bought the CHLPP program and members and merged them into Patriot Legal....CHLPP is the membership I used to suggest to my clients (they were around before CCW Safe) and they acted just like CCW Safe does now.

So why don't I recommend Patriot Legal to my clients?

Well...Patriot legal seems like a great organization and they do pay for your legal fees if you are involved in a Self-Defense shooting – BUT – As of October 2014, they do NOT pay for your Expert Witness testimony and this could cost you ten's of thousands of dollars if you go to trial. I'm not sure why they do not offer this coverage but for now I cannot recommend them when CCW Safe provides what it provides.

Don't get me wrong, Patriot Legal is still better than a sharp stick in the eye...it's just not as comprehensive as CCW Safe. I said I would rank these in the order I suggest them and Patriot comes in at #2 for Criminal Legal Defense protection.

To get your Patriot Legal membership please visit www.patriotlegalprotection.com

US Law Shield

This is a smaller group that only offers protection in 13 states and is very similar to Patriot Legal. They also do not pay for Expert Witness testimony and they are double the cost of Patriot Legal...again they are better than a stick in the eye but I think you get my point.

To get your US Law Shield membership please visit www.USlawshield.com

Armed Citizen Legal Defense Network

This is a program that again is better than being poked in the eye but I can't recommend this one either...you get money for an attorney right away to get you through the initial days after the shooting but after that you have to appeal for more grants if your case is going forward...not bad if you get them but why screw around?

So to sum this part up: Just get yourself a CCW Safe membership and rest easy at night.

To get your Armed Citizen Legal Defense Network membership please visit www.armedcitizensnetwork.org

Author's note: *I am in no way affiliated with CCW Safe nor am I paid to endorse their organization. It just makes the most sense to have their membership!*

CHAPTER 2

THE preferred program for Concealed Carry and Self Defense

continued

LIABILITY COVERAGE FOR CIVIL SUIT PROTECTION

IMPORTANT NOTE

You do NOT need to be a Concealed Carry Permit/License holder to have this type of Civil Suit protection discussed in this part of the insurance program...If you own a gun (shotgun, deer rifle, etc.) you need to have coverage with a Self-Defense friendly insurance carrier in the event you use your gun to defend you or your family in your home! Remember, if you own a gun you need the right coverage!

We have the criminal defense legal fee side covered for Concealed Carry Permit/License holders which some would argue is the most important part...you don't want to spend time in prison for a Self-Defense incident if at all possible and I would have to agree...BUT...you can't forget the other side of the equation.

Being cleared of criminal charges for a Self-Defense shooting is a great relief but what happens if you are sued by your target, their family OR even worse... an innocent bystander to the shooting who was wounded or their family if by chance they were killed by your actions? The weight of a several hundred thousand to possibly a Million Dollar or more lawsuit against you will surely cause some sleepless nights if you do not have insurance in place to protect you.

I mean really...how could being involved in a shooting put me at risk?

CHAPTER 2

What about the Castle Doctrine? I'm allowed to defend myself without being charged or sued right?

Well, yes and no...let's take my example I used in the Criminal Defense Legal Fee Membership section again and apply it to the Civil Suit side of the equation:

You are carrying your weapon concealed and you stop to get gas and a cup of coffee on the way to work. While inside a gunman rushes in and not seeing you, points his gun at the cashier and asks for money...as you are backing away slowly to get to a safer position, he sees you, swings the gun on you, you feel threatened and you shoot the guy...

Self-Defense? Most likely...are you immune from being sued by the perpetrator? *Maybe, maybe not...*

Here's the big problem with the Castle Doctrine language here in Wisconsin and it is similar in other parts of the country as well. You are immune from prosecution or lawsuits when you defend yourself in your HOME, AUTO or BUSINESS. In my example above you are in none of the three and as such, if the perpetrator wanted to bring a lawsuit against you he could...and you'd be on your own to defend yourself.

Do you have $5,000, $10,000, $20,000 or more to defend yourself if you do not have an insurance carrier there to protect you? I have the money but I wouldn't be happy about paying it out that's for sure!

Would you win or get the case thrown out? Maybe...probably...but how much did it cost you out of pocket? If you have Self-Defense friendly language in your policy, your insurance company steps up to defend you and you don't have to worry about paying for the defense.

Now let's look at what happens in this horrific turn of events:

*You are carrying your weapon concealed and you stop to get gas and a cup of coffee on the way to work. While inside a gunman rushes in and not seeing you, points his gun at the cashier and asks for money...as you are backing away slowly to get to a safer position, he sees you, swings the gun on you, you feel threatened and you shoot the guy...**and the bullet goes through him...hits the door jamb and ricochets off and hits the cashier...paralyzing him for life or even killing him.***

Are you protected by the Castle Doctrine? *No...*

Are you on the hook for a lawsuit to pay medical bills, loss of use of their limbs or even the loss of a loved-one? *Very likely...*

If you have assets (home, autos, and investments...anything of value) they can be exposed to a judgment from a lawsuit in this instance.

Would you want to have an insurance policy that has Self-Defense friendly language in it if this happened to you? Would you want at least $1,000,000 or more in coverage? I'm guessing you think like I do and the answer is YES...

We do not carry a weapon or use one for Self-Defense lightly...we know there is a great responsibility in doing so and the last thing we want to do is shoot someone...but if it comes down to him or you...you are going to fight to protect yourself at all costs...the time to think about what happens in a worst-case scenario is not AFTER you were in a shooting but now...before anything happens...you prepare for the worst and hope for the best...you are smart about owning or carrying a gun.

As Attorney Paul Bucher said in his interview, being involved in a shooting is a very traumatic incident...and the last thing you need to worry about is defending yourself against a Civil Suit. My theory about insurance is; **"it is better to have it and not need it than to need it and not have it"** and quite frankly it is very easy to get the proper coverage in place when you have a knowledgeable agent that understands what you need – like me!

The solution:

As I mentioned earlier in the book, there are several carriers or programs that offer coverage against Civil Suits stemming from a Self-Defense shooting. In my opinion the BEST option for gun owners and obviously CCW Permit holders is to have at least $1,000,000 in protection with a Personal Liability Umbrella policy, if not more. Of the options available for civil suit protections, the Personal Liability Umbrella offers the highest limits and the most protection – and better yet it even protects you for non Self-Defense incidents (car crashes, etc.).

Let me explain what an Umbrella is and does for you and why everyone should have one...

A Personal Liability Umbrella policy or "Excess Liability" policy is designed to be essentially what the name states...just like a rain umbrella covers over everything underneath it to protect it from falling rain or snow; a Liability Umbrella policy sits over your other insurance policies to add a protective layer of "extra liability" coverage for you and your family.

For example, you will have either a home (or renter's/condo) policy, an auto policy, possibly a boat, motorcycle, ATV or even Snowmobile policy that all have some level of Liability Coverage in them for your protection from negligent acts (car, boat or ATV crashes caused by you or someone tripping, falling and injuring themselves at your home). If you are sued from an act like this the liability portion of the policy that covers the incident in question is the primary coverage.

If you have Auto limits of $250,000/$500,000 that means you have Bodily Injury Liability coverage of $250,000 per person up to $500,000 per accident for lawsuits and injuries arising out of an accident caused by you. If you have a $1,000,000 Personal Liability Umbrella policy you will now have extra liability coverage over your auto policy so in an accident you really would have $1,250,000 per person up to $1,500,000 per accident if there is more than one injured party for coverage...which is by far MUCH better.

The benefit of a Personal Liability Umbrella policy is that they are a very cheap alternative to adding extra liability coverage. In my home state of Wisconsin I can add a $1,000,000 Umbrella for as little as $70 per year...and oh by the way...**the umbrella also covers you for Self-Defense incidents!**

Let me explain how the Self-Defense coverage works with the Umbrella coverage in almost every case: Very few carriers have a home policy with Self-Defense friendly language in it...so with one of these carriers, a Self-Defense incident that happens in your home would have the Homeowner's Policy become the primary policy that has Self-Defense coverage and the Umbrella becomes Secondary Coverage over and above the liability limits in the Homeowner's Policy.

If the Self-Defense incident happens outside the home, your Homeowner's Policy would most-likely not offer coverage and your Umbrella Policy now becomes the Primary Coverage. In almost all instances of Self-Defense, there will be no underlying coverage for Self-Defense in any of your policies, so the Umbrella Policy which is usually secondary coverage, becomes primary coverage for that incident.

Confused? Don't be...just know that if you are involved in a Self-Defense incident and your Umbrella Policy has the Self-Defense friendly language in it, that carrier will look at the underlying policies to see if any of them will offer primary coverage for you. If not, they become the primary coverage and will defend you against the lawsuit and pay for an attorney to defend you and the insurance company against the suit.

For quotes you can call our office at **608-663-9800** or better yet visit our website at **www.ConcealedCarryInsurance.com** and fill out our information request form.

What makes my carriers different?

In my research of Self-Defense Insurance, I found several Home & Auto Insurance Carriers that were "Self-Defense Friendly" in their policy language. Being an Independent Insurance Agent, I quickly contracted with several carriers who have the correct language so I can protect my gun-owning clients against Self-Defense incidents...and I am looking to add several more. *(I need to give credit to Gene German here who is a CCW trainer up in MN – without him I'm sure it would have taken me much, much longer to figure this stuff out...Thanks Gene!)*

So...what is it exactly that makes the policy language I use "Self-Defense Friendly?" As most every agent knows, liability policies will always have some sort of exclusion from coverage for "Intentional Injuries or Intentional Acts" or some variation thereof. Meaning if you do something like pull the trigger of a gun on purpose to shoot someone, it is an intentional act and will be excluded.

I found the policy language with the carriers I use that adds back coverage for Self-Defense in their Policies...crucial language that ALL GUN OWNERS should have!

Because there is no set standard policy form for all insurance carriers, many policies vary in their language and it is very hard for me to list all the variations here in the book. The biggest thing you need to look for is in the Exclusions section of the policy they add back coverage for the protection of person or property.

Again, there are many different policy forms so be sure to read your policy carefully...the language would be in the section that excludes intentional injuries and/or intentional acts...it will say *"however we do allow for the protection of person or property"* or some variation of that language in this section if they do allow it... and that is the Self-Defense coverage.

If you'd like to see if you have coverage or not with your current policy, you can give our office a call at **608-663-9800** and we will happily review your policy with you.

WARNING!!!
This is the number one mistake 99.99% of all agents make

They assume their company's Umbrella Policy will cover you in the event of a Self-Defense incident without ever asking or understanding it...leaving YOU open to lawsuits because they didn't take the time to research their policy language thoroughly. Don't trust your agent...**it could cost you Hundreds of Thousands of Dollars or More!**

I have seen it happen numerous times...the biggest culprits in my area are the American Family Insurance agents. They tell their clients they would be covered for Self-Defense...not even knowing their policies exclude coverage for these acts AND their company has come out on record stating they won't cover acts of Self-Defense....see the story that was in the Milwaukee Journal Sentinel on our website at **www.ConcealedCarryInsurance.com** and read it for yourself.

Our Insurance Agency is different...obviously you know by now I understand what it takes to have the proper coverage for Self-Defense. When you call our office for a review of your current coverage/company and we find you do have coverage we'll tell you...and make sure you have the proper limits in place for your situation with your carrier.

If we find that you do not have coverage (or even if you do) and you would like to have a competitive quote from the premier Self-Defense Insurance Agency in the country, we'd be happy to help you with your coverage needs.

For quotes you can call our office at **608-663-9800** or better yet visit our website at **www.ConcealedCarryInsurance.com** and fill out our information request form.

The only drawback (which isn't even a drawback) is that you can't get a Personal Liability Umbrella as a single stand-alone policy...you have to have either your home, autos or both with the carrier to be able to add the Umbrella to your coverage. Yes, you can move just one of your policies to one of our carriers but I don't recommend it...I don't like to be a part-time agent...it makes it hard for me to give you the best service and coverage possible — plus you lose out on the auto/home discounts when you combine them under one carrier.

** UPDATED **

As of August 2014, I do have a stand alone umbrella policy available that has self-defense friendly language in it!

Many people are reluctant to switch insurance companies and I can appreciate that...loyalty is hard to come by these days...BUT...protection matters more than loyalty when it comes to Self-Defense coverage — *doesn't it?*

I have had many clients say they do not want to leave their current agent or insurance company but after a few days (and a few sleepless nights) of thinking about what could happen after they have talked to me – they have decided to switch their insurance to a Self-Defense friendly carrier!

The funny thing is – more often than not we are able to offer our clients better coverage with Self-Defense friendly policy language for less than they are paying with their current insurance companies!

That's the benefit of using an Independent Insurance Agent who can shop around for you...and when you get an agent who is a Second Amendment supporter that understands what you as a gun owner or Concealed Carry Permit holder needs to protect you and your family in the worst-case scenario – *you can sleep better at night knowing you have an insurance company and agent who have your back!*

So you know you need to have a Self-Defense friendly insurance carrier backing you...what do you do next?

You schedule a coverage review with our office to see if you have coverage with your current carrier or not. If not, you give us the information for your FREE no-obligation quotes...AND THEN YOU DECIDE! Don't make up your mind you are not going to switch companies before you have reviewed all the information.

For quotes you can call our office at **608-663-9800** or better yet visit our website at www.ConcealedCarryInsurance.com and fill out our information request form.

CHAPTER 3

The United States Concealed Carry Association

— SELF DEFENSE SHIELD —

I just discussed what I feel is the absolute BEST option when it comes to legal fee and civil suit protection with our customized protection program using the CCW Safe legal fee membership and having a comprehensive insurance program that includes a Personal Umbrella policy that has Self-Defense friendly language in it (See Chapter 2).

But what if for some reason you absolutely cannot or will not switch your home or auto insurance (or both) to a Self-Defense friendly insurance carrier like the ones we use for our gun-owning clients? I do get a little resistance from people at times who feel this way (although they usually change their thinking after a few days, weeks or even months of it gnawing at them) and they always ask what their other options are.

In this chapter I will talk about two other options that give you some Civil Suit protection as well as reimbursement for legal fees paid for a criminal defense for a Self-Defense shooting. Note I said *reimbursement for legal fees*...with these plans you would have to pay to defend yourself and then once you are cleared of any criminal wrongdoing you will be reimbursed for your legal fees paid.

Contrast this with the CCW Safe program which pays your legal fees for you on your behalf and it isn't quite as good BUT it's better than nothing! I actually recommend to people who do not want the full protection of a Personal Liability Umbrella to get a CCW Safe membership as well as one of these memberships to give them better coverage than just these two programs alone.

The program I am talking about in this chapter is:

- The United States Concealed Carry Association – Self Defense Shield

Now, to be fair, this program is more than just an insurance policy...it is a membership organization that just happens to provide other benefits of membership.

The USCCA is a membership organization for Concealed Carry Permit/License holders and they provide a really nice magazine each month in the US Mail along with email updates and an online interactive website with all kinds of great content. I personally belong to the USCCA to take advantage of their great content and Tim Schmidt who founded the organization is a great guy and really knows his stuff. The articles in the monthly magazine are great and I learn new stuff all the time!

Membership will give you the benefit of an included insurance program and depending on what level of membership you have, you could receive up to a $1,000,000 Civil Liability policy that has up to $100,000 worth of legal fee reimbursement. Again, not quite as good as the package I have put together for our gun-owning clients but better than nothing...

www.ConcealedCarryInsurance.com/Resources

CHAPTER 3

The following information helps explain the benefit of membership in USCCA at: https://www.usconcealedcarry.com/

The USCCA Inc. has your solution to this incredibly difficult problem in our brand new, insurance-backed membership benefit called Self-Defense SHIELD. If you're forced to justifiably use your gun in self-defense, Self-Defense SHIELD will help pay for your expert pro-2nd Amendment lawyer by reimbursing your legal-defense expenses following your acquittal - an ingenious system critical to the arsenal of any responsibly armed citizen.

From now on, being a USCCA Inc. member will mean you can carry your gun confidently without having to fear losing EVERYTHING else when you're forced to use it.

When you use your handgun to defend your family, instead of being subjected to the mercy of the courts like a penniless puppet, you'll have the power that comes with a strong, reputable attorney, and a support network that will never abandon you when you need it the most.

Imagine this: You have successfully defended yourself in a near-death gunfight brought on by a violent felon looking to kill you for the wallet in your pocket, or for a chance to have his way with your family...

As devastating as it would be to have to use your gun in self defense, how terrible would it be to have the legal system that you've obeyed and respected for your whole life suddenly turn against you, and try to paint you as a murderer?

Unbelievable? It happens every day.

In fact, men are sitting in prison right now for defending their families from violent attackers hell-bent on ending lives. WHY are they sitting in prison? Why are most people who use a weapon to defend themselves painted as murderers and trigger happy maniacs in court? The answer is simple: because they COULDN'T AFFORD A GOOD LAWYER.

And in America, it's no secret that Justice ALWAYS goes to the highest bidder. (Just ask OJ Simpson).

Now, I personally would rather defend my wife and children from the attack of some ruthless thug and sit in prison for the rest of my life than the alternative of letting the bastard have his way with my family... But NEITHER of those are REAL options for me.

I want to be able to exercise my God-given right of self-defense when I am threatened, and I DO NOT want to be judged a criminal for doing so!

It is VERY expensive to hire a good lawyer in that event (as much as $150,000 or more), so I started looking for an insurance policy to cover my self-defense shooting lawyer costs.

I hoped to find an insurance policy that would cover me if I ever needed a lawyer. After all, I've got car insurance... getting "lawyer insurance" seemed like a natural next step to me!

Here was the problem- that insurance policy didn't exist! There were a couple options out therefore individually under-written policies, but I quickly realized... I would have to be an idiot to have this kind of insurance policy. The reason is, when you're the policy holder, that's seen as equity, and it opens you up to a LOT of liability.

So I asked myself (and anyone that would listen): What if there was a way you could have insurance-backed benefits (like $150,000 of complete attorney coverage), WITHOUT taking out an insurance policy?

I've spent a better part of the last year working with dozens of lawyers and insurance companies, and we've finally created a solution that will give any law-abiding citizen who responsibly defends himself and his family a fighting chance in court.

I can't describe the horror I would feel after defending my wife and three children against two home invaders or a back-alley thug, only to go to prison and leave them without a husband, father, and primary source of income.

I can't imagine being thrown into an 8'x8' cell with some unscrupulous low-life rapist or murderer.

I can't describe the anguish of imagining my friends and family turning against me after some judge and jury decide that my action to stop a vicious felon in his tracks was not justified... and that instead of defending myself from a violent attacker, I had (in the court's eyes), murdered a man. This is NOT acceptable.

The fact is I NEVER want to be forced to give up control over my fate because I can't afford a good lawyer. I NEVER want to lose my freedom, and force my wife and kids to try to survive without me. I NEVER want to find myself thrown into an unfriendly legal battle with NO support network.

And I NEVER want the good and honorable members of the USCCA Inc. to go through such a horrifying experience either. I want YOU to have the best self defense lawyers watching your back, and I want you to be free from worrying about how you're going to be able to afford them, and I want you to be able to go on with your life after being forced to defend your family.

The brand-new Self-Defense SHIELD benefit of a USCCA Inc. PLUS membership takes care of ALL that.

A gunfight is bad enough. You should NOT be punished for doing the right thing.

Self-Defense SHIELD solves a HUGE problem for you, and that is "When I need to use my firearm for self defense... how am I going to pay for a good lawyer?"

If you're forced to justifiably use your gun in self-defense, Self-Defense SHIELD will help pay for your expert pro-2nd Amendment lawyer by reimbursing your legal-defense expenses following your acquittal - an ingenious system critical to the arsenal of any responsibly armed citizen.

Author's Note: As I said previously, the USCCA is much more than an insurance policy so please check out what they have to offer.

****Please note, the USCCA is the one who holds the insurance policy and you as a member are given benefits from the policy – see the website for more information.****

www.ConcealedCarryInsurance.com/Resources

Here are the levels of membership for the USCCA and the insurance benefits provided as listed on their website:

Silver Plus Membership
$250,000 for Civil Suits
$50,000 for Criminal Defense reimbursement

Gold Plus Membership
$500,000 for Civil Suits
$75,000 for Criminal Defense reimbursement

Platinum Plus Membership
$1,000,000 for Civil Suits
$100,000 for Criminal Defense reimbursement

This information is provided as information only – please click on the link to visit the website for more information.

Again, the USCCA is a great organization for Concealed Carry Permit/License holders and if you are one of them please check them out today.

CHAPTER 4

The Lochton Risk Program

- ENDORSED BY THE NRA -

http://www.locktonrisk.com/nrains/defense.htm

The National Rifle Association does not offer an insurance policy for Self-Defense directly but they do endorse the Lochton Risk Program for their members.

Remember when I started listing the available insurance packages or programs I listed them in order starting with what I feel is the best coverage and am working backwards listing lesser coverage plans. Being back here in the "rear with the gear" should tell you that although this program is better than nothing, it offers less coverage than previously mentioned insurance programs.

The Lochton Risk program is in my mind a lesser program because it has less coverage available than the others. I'm not passing judgment on the NRA or the Lochton Risk program in any way — I believe in insurance so again this plan would be better than no plan for you.

Here's some information from the Lochton Risk website on their program:

http://www.locktonrisk.com/nrains/defense.htm

Self-Defense Coverage

Our Self-Defense Insurance protects National Rifle Association members who need extra protection not found in most homeowners' policies. The coverage is a rider to the Excess Personal Liability coverage, and provides civil defense and liability and criminal defense reimbursement if you are involved in an act of self-defense.

What's Covered:

- Provides coverage up to the limit selected for criminal and civil defense costs.
- Cost of civil suit defense is provided in addition to the limit of liability for bodily injury and property damage.
- Criminal Defense Reimbursement is provided for alleged criminal actions involving self-defense when you are acquitted of such criminal charges or the charges are dropped.

Liability Limit Options:

- $100,000 Combined Single Limit with $50,000 criminal defense reimbursement sub-limit
- $250,000 Combined Single Limit with $50,000 criminal defense reimbursement sub-limit
- 500,000 Combined Single Limit with $100,000 criminal defense reimbursement sub-limit
- $1,000,000 Combined Single Limit with $100,000 criminal defense reimbursement sub-limit

---

You can probably figure out this is a lesser program because it allows up to $1.000,000 for civil liability protection and an additional sub-limit up to $100,000 reimbursement for criminal defense coverage. Again this is better than nothing.

It also costs about the same as using our preferred package of the CCW Safe membership combined with a Personal Liability Umbrella policy...on average our package's extra costs are the same as both the Lochton program AND the USCCA's top membership level...which is why I feel the package I put together for my clients is the best...more and better coverage for the same money!!!

CHAPTER 5

Second Defense Alliance

www.MySecondDefenseAlliance.com

1-855-FOR-SDA1 (1-855-367-7321)

There is another program that is worth mentioning that is geared towards Self-Defense in your home and that is the Second Defense Alliance. Being all over page 1 of Google when you search Concealed Carry Insurance I was contacted by them about their program and it just so happened I was writing this book so I told them I would include their program.

Here is some information on what they do from a brochure they produced:

What Constitutes a Home Invasion?

While home invasion is not a legally defined federal offense throughout the United States, it's generally defined as an unauthorized, forceful entry into a dwelling, with violent intent to commit a crime against the occupants.

It's our sincere hope you never need the assurance our membership provides. But if you do, know we stand with you to protect your rights, your well-being and your liberty.

Membership Benefits

When help is needed, it's needed right away—not after all your legal issues have been settled. Our members receive up to $50,000 in financial assistance immediately for:

- Expert legal defense
- Bail bond premium, up to $4,500
- Injuries sustained in the home invasion, up to $10,000
- Six one hour counseling sessions (more upon approval)
- Emergency medical expenses, up to $10,000

More benefits listed on the website

www.MySecondDefenseAlliance.com

After a home invasion shooting occurs, arriving police officers often create an overwhelming show of force to restore order and establish control. At this point, things can get pretty strange.

Even though you've simply defended yourself and your family, you may be treated like a suspect instead of a victim—disarmed, handcuffed and even arrested. You or your family may also need emergency medical attention. Later, counseling may be necessary to heal lingering emotional wounds.

SDA provides immediate support—arranging legal counsel, posting bond money if needed. We will help cover hospital expenses, emergency medical care, and arrange qualified counseling sessions for individuals or families.

We will do what it takes to protect you, so you have the reassurance you need to protect your family.

Second Defense Alliance's website provides you and your family with all the resources you need in the event of a home invasion self-defense shooting

On Our Emergency Help Page you'll Find Links To:

- Legal counsel
- Medical support
- Therapy services
- Our FAQ page answers questions on
- Home defense
- Gun ownership guidelines
- Membership services questions
- Membership benefits and more
- Visit the news and events page for updates on
- Recent home invasion stories in the news
- Policy updates on home defense law
- The latest trends in gun ownership laws

To enroll in Second Defense Alliance, visit our website:

www.MySecondDefenseAlliance.com and apply for your membership. Within twenty four hours, you'll receive an email updating you on your SDA membership status.

Membership Plans

Our memberships are very affordable, starting as low as $10 per month. Payment may be made in installments, or paid up front. Call **1-855-FOR-SDA1 (1-855-367-7321)** or visit our website for details.

- $131 One Year Membership
  (or two semi-annual payments of $69)
- $250 Two Year Membership
- $350 Three Year Membership

We'll do what it takes to protect you, so you have the peace of mind and tranquility of knowing that you have the support you will need by your side when an incident occurs.

A professional English-speaking resolution specialist will take your secured information and follow up with you promptly.

Membership approval subject to verification of registered gun ownership by U.S. Bureau of Alcohol, Tobacco, Firearms and Explosives. Registration is automatic with the purchase of a firearm from a registered Federal Firearms Licensed Dealer (FFLD). If this information is not on file at the time of the incident, proof of registration may be confirmed with a copy of your sales receipt from a registered FFLD.

This plan is geared more towards the gun owner and not necessarily for Concealed Carry Permit/License holders and it appears they have put together a nice package. Give them a call if you have questions or visit their website for more information.

CHAPTER 6

My Final Thoughts

Well...that's it for now, although I have a sneaking suspicion this won't be the last of it. This has been an ever-changing journey for me over the last three-plus years and I'm sure there will be new and improved information that will need to be considered in the coming months and years.

I hope after reading this book you realize that owning and carrying weapons is a very serious proposition and should not be taken lightly. Nobody EVER wants to have to use a weapon but in this crazy world we live in it is our duty to take the protection of ourselves and our loved ones into our own hands when the situation requires it....and if that happens you want to make sure you have the proper legal fee and civil suit protection in place BEFORE it happens!

I take it for granted you already know this but I'll point it out anyway...you can't buy insurance for something that has already happened...meaning if you are involved in a Self-Defense shooting you can't get a CCW Safe membership quickly to pay your legal fees. Just like most health insurance won't cover a pre-existing condition, a Self-Defense incident will be along the same lines. You have to have coverage in place before it ever happens if you want to have it covered under your insurance program. Don't put it off any longer...

I said in my introduction I believe in insurance...what would you expect? I'm an insurance guy! But seriously, my philosophy is "it's better to have it and not need it than to need it and not have it." For the cost of a cup of coffee per day on average you can have insurance protection for you and your family...your assets...your future...everything you've worked so hard to acquire in your life!

I strongly suggest you visit my website or call my office to request a comprehensive insurance package review so you know you'll have the coverage you need and you can sleep better at night...I believe in what I have put together for my clients and yes, I have the same insurance package already set up for myself that I would put together for you...I practice what I preach!

I am the only insurance agent in the country who has taken the time to figure out what we Concealed Carry Permit/License holders and gun owners need for insurance protection and I'm proud to say I am the #1 Leading Expert in this insurance niche and I want to help fellow gun owners protect themselves.

You can visit my website by going to **www.ConcealedCarryInsurance.com** or call my office at **608-663-9800**.

Whatever you do, use this information wisely and take action now with one of these programs...and PLEASE tell every Concealed Carry Permit/License holder and gun owner you know about this book and this information...there are Millions of gun owners in this country who have no idea the insurance program they currently have will probably not protect them against a Self-Defense incident!

RESOURCES

Where is your license / permit valid?

View the handgun laws in all 50 states, see where your license or permit is acceptable (and be sure to sign up for automatic updates to the page).
http://www.handgunlaw.us/

Where can you carry openly?

http://opencarry.org/

Attorney information - Wisconsin

Attorney Paul Bucher - Milwaukee area
http://www.bucherlawgroup.com/

Attorney Mark Hinkston - Milwaukee area
http://www.avvo.com/attorneys/53406-wi-mark-hinkston-1522979.html

Chris Van Wagner - Madison area
http://www.vanwagnerwood.com/

Gun-Friendly Organizations

Second Amendment Foundation
http://www.saf.org/

National Rifle Association
http://home.nra.org/#

United States Concealed Carry Association
https://www.usconcealedcarry.com/

Wisconsin Carry Inc.
http://www.wisconsincarry.org/default.html#

FFL Gun Dealer Locator

http://fflgundealers.net/
http://www.fflregistry.com/

Insurance Providers for Concealed Carry & Self-Defense

Affordable Insurance Solutions LLC
www.ConcealedCarryInsurance.com

United States Concealed Carry Association
https://www.usconcealedcarry.com/

The NRA endorsed Lochton Risk Program
http://www.locktonrisk.com/nrains/defense.htm

www.ingramcontent.com/pod-product-compliance
Lightning Source LLC
Chambersburg PA
CBHW070940280326
41934CB00009B/1951

* 9 7 8 0 5 7 8 1 2 0 3 5 5 *